Essential Histories

The Russian Civil War
1918–22

Essential Histories

The Russian Civil War
1918–22

David Bullock

First published in 2008 by Osprey Publishing,
Midland House, West Way, Botley, Oxford OX2 0PH, UK
44-02 23rd St, Suite 219, Long Island City, NY 11101, USA
Email: info@ospreypublishing.com

ISBN: 978 1 84603 271 4

Page layout by Ken Vail Graphic Design, Cambridge, UK
Typeset in Monotype Gill Sans and ITC Stone Serif
Cartography by The Map Studio
Index by Fineline Editorial services
Origination by PPS Grasmere, Leeds, UK
Printed and bound in China through Bookbuilders

10 11 12 13 14   12 11 10 9 8 7 6 5 4 3

A CIP catalogue record for this book is available from the
British Library.

FOR A CATALOGUE OF ALL BOOKS PUBLISHED BY OSPREY MILITARY
AND AVIATION PLEASE CONTACT:

Osprey Direct, c/o Random House Distribution Center,
400 Hahn Road, Westminster, MD 21157
Email: uscustomerservice@ospreypublishing.com

Osprey Direct, The Book Service Ltd, Distribution Centre,
Colchester Road, Frating Green, Colchester, Essex, CO7 7DW
Email: customerservice@ospreypublishing.com

www.ospreypublishing.com

Contents

The former Russian Empire in the national flag colours of red, blue and white. Overhead, the state crown is surrounded by a wreath of thorns symbolizing suffering and sacrifice. The imperial eagle has been replaced by a black eagle with sword and extended talons that spreads the red cloak of communism over the land. (*Chasevoi émigré* journal, 1933)

Introduction

The Russian Civil War of 1918–22 arose out of the cataclysmic events of World War One. This civil war dwarfed all others of the 20th century in scope and significance. The lives of tens of millions were lost or changed forever in the ensuing conflagration – from battle, disease, famine, imprisonment, execution, dislocation and exile.

New weapons of war emerged. The aeroplane, armoured car, tank and armoured train were tested over the vast expanses of Russia, the largest country in the world, in a war of mobility not seen on the relatively static fronts that characterized World War One. Even so, the older weapons of war remained. This was the last war in which cavalry armies duelled en masse, sword on lance. Bugles still rang and unfurled flags fluttered above infantry charging into the steel mouths of guns.

More than two dozen countries took part in these torturous years of civil war. Peripheral regions of the former Russian Empire that had broken away to form new nations had to fight for independence: Finland, Poland, Estonia, Lithuania, Latvia, Belarus, Ukraine, Georgia and Azerbaijan. Other countries directly intervened in the conflict as a consequence of events arising out of World War One, including Great Britain, France, Italy, Canada, Japan, Germany, Austria-Hungary, Romania, Greece, the Ottoman Empire and the United States.

Still others participated in the fighting because their troops were trapped inside Russia at the end of World War One, such as Serbia and Czechoslovakia, or fought because

Kiev, capital of the Ukraine. Note the Nicholas (chain) Bridge in the background. The city changed hands 19 times during the civil war. (Bullock collection)

the civil war spilled over into their territory, for example, Mongolia and China. At the end, the maps of northeastern and eastern Europe, the Caucasus, Central Asia and the Far East had to be redrawn.

Historiography poses the question – 'when did the Russian Civil War begin?' Historians, authors, politicians and diplomats have had their own points of view depending on when their country or party interest became involved, or to stress a particular methodology or ideological line of argument. This book's position is that the era of the Provisional Government, from April to November 1917, was a time of transition between the fall of the tsar and the outbreak of civil war. Civil war began when an organized opposition sought to overturn the October Revolution of 1917. In this context, civil war began when notable White generals formed the Volunteer Army in South Russia in November/December 1917. However, that force did not engage in significant military action until the opening days of 1918.

The question 'when did the civil war end?' is equally problematical. The majority of Whites on the Southern Front thought the conflict ended in November 1920 after defeat in the Crimea and exile. Whites in the Northern and Northwestern Fronts had already accepted defeat that February. Whites in the Far East continued battle actions until 1922, notwithstanding one final act of quixotic desperation in Yakutsk in spring 1923.

For many Reds, the civil war certainly ended in 1922, after the last of the major peasant and internal rebellions had been fully crushed and after the last of the foreign interventionists left Russian soil. However, spasmodic resistance occurred in the Ukraine, the Caucasus, Central Asia and the Far East well into the 1920s.

Red victory in the Russian Civil War unleashed the new doctrine of communism with its concept of international revolution upon the world. This set the stage for the Cold War that began in the late 1940s and which divided the world into two armed political camps, communist and anti-communist. But this path, of course, was never certain, for the outcome could only be decided in the severe trials of civil war.

Chronology

(Dates are given in Western, Gregorian calendar style and are 13 days ahead of Eastern or Julian calendar style. The following represents only a few of the important dates in this momentous period.)

1917 **7 March** Start of February Revolution
15 March Tsar Nicholas II abdicates
15 March Formation of Provisional Government
16 April Lenin returns to Russia
3 May Demonstrations in Petrograd (formally St Petersburg but the name was changed during World War One to sound less German)
18 May Provisional Government reorganizes
2 July July Offensive begins
16–18 July July Days – attempted Bolshevik coup
21 July Alexander Kerensky becomes prime minister of Provisional Government
1 August General Lavr Kornilov becomes commander-in-chief
6–14 September Kornilov attempts to restore order
6 October Leon Trotsky becomes chairman of the Petrograd Soviet
25 October Formation of the Military Revolutionary Committee
7 November October Revolution begins
13 November Kerensky's counter-revolution fails
15 November Mikhail Alexiev establishes the Volunteer Army in the Don
20 November Central Rada declares Ukrainian independence
2 December Generals Kornilov, Denikin, Romanovsky, Lukomsky and Markov escape from Bykhov and head for the Don

6 December Finland declares independence
20 December Establishment of the Cheka
22 December Peace negotiations begin at Brest-Litovsk

1918 **12 January** Latvia declares independence from Russia
19 January Bolsheviks shut down Constituent Assembly
8 February Red Army takes Kiev
9 February Ukrainian Rada makes peace with Central Powers
14 February Soviet Russia adopts the Western or Gregorian calendar
14 February Grigori Semenov raises army in Trans-Baikal region
16 February Lithuania declares independence
19 February Central Powers advance through Ukraine
22 February Volunteer Army evacuates Rostov-on-Don and begins 'Ice March'
24 February Estonia declares independence
25 February Don Cossack Front collapses under General A. Kaledin
2 March Germans enter Kiev
3 March Treaty of Brest-Litovsk signed
12 March Bolsheviks move government and capital from Petrograd to Moscow
14 March Red Army captures Ekaterinodar
3 April German forces land in Finland
4 April British landings begin in Siberia
5 April Initial landing of the Allies at Murmansk

The strategic railway junction at Kharkov through which
Denikin's Armed Forces of South Russia advanced on
Moscow in 1919. (Bullock collection)

5 April Germans take Kharkov
6 April Japanese land in Vladivostok
13 April Kornilov killed at
Ekaterinodar
13 April Bolsheviks begin crackdown
on Anarchists
13 April Central Powers occupy
Odessa
29 April Pavel Skoropadsky
establishes the Hetmanate under
German sponsorship
6 May Don Cossacks retake
Novocherkassk, the Don capital
8 May Germans enter
Rostov-on-Don
11 May Petr Krasnov elected
Ataman of Don Cossacks
25 May Czech Legion revolts
against Bolsheviks
26 May Georgia declares
independence
29–30 May Czechs take Penza
and Syzran
1 June Provisional Government of
Siberia established at Omsk

8 June Czechs capture Samara,
People's Government forms
3 June Allies reinforce Murmansk
23 June Czech Legion takes Ufa
14 July Anti-Bolshevik forces
established at Ashkhabad and
Trans-Caspian region
16 July Execution of the tsar and
royal family at Ekaterinburg
21 July Socialist Revolutionary revolt
at Yaroslavl crushed
25 July Czech Legion captures
Ekaterinburg
2 August Anti-Bolshevik forces take
control of Archangel
3 August Allies land in Archangel
3 August Americans land at
Vladivostok
4 August British land at Baku
6 August Czech and KOMUCH forces
seize Kazan
14 August British Dunsterforce
arrives in Baku
15 August Volunteer Army takes
Ekaterinodar
26 August Volunteer Army enters
Novorossisk
4 September Americans arrive
at Archangel

St Petersburg, the tsars' capital and scene of the Bolsheviks' first triumphs. (© Corbis)

10 September Red Army captures Kazan

23 September All Russian Provisional Government (Directory) established at Ufa

8 October Red Army enters Samara

15 October Krasnov advances on Tsaritsyn

29–30 October Narva, Pskov fall to Red Army

11 November Armistice ending World War One signed

11 November Poland declares independence

18 November Alexander Kolchak becomes Supreme Ruler at Omsk

18 November Latvia declares independence from all powers

14 December Collapse of Skoropadsky's Hetmanate

17 December French intervention in Odessa

25 December Perm falls to Kolchak

1919   **3 January** Red Army takes Kharkov and Riga

6 January Kiev falls to the Reds

15 February Anton Denikin becomes commander-in-chief, Armed Forces of South Russia (AFSR)

13 March Kolchak's Whites begin spring offensive

5 April British end intervention in the Trans-Caspian

8 April French end intervention in Odessa

19 May AFSR begins spring offensive

23 May German 'Iron Division' and Whites take Riga

27 June Denikin captures Kharkov

2 July Wrangel takes Tsaritsyn

15 July Ashkhabad falls to the Reds

21 July Red Army takes Perm

25 July Red Army enters Chelyabinsk

19 August British evacuate Baku and Azerbaijan

23 August AFSR takes Odessa

31 August AFSR takes Kiev

20 September AFSR takes Kursk

26 September Nestor Makhno defeats Whites at Peregonovka

27 September Allies evacuate Archangel

28 September Northwestern Army advances on Petrograd

30 September Allies evacuate Archangel
6 October Don Army takes Voronezh
12 October Allies evacuate Murmansk
14 October AFSR takes Orel
24 October Orel falls to the Reds, Cossacks abandon Voronezh
9 November Makhno captures Ekaterinoslav
11 November Cossacks defeated at Kastornaya
14 November Omsk falls to the Reds
12 December Kharkov falls to the Reds
16 December Kiev falls to the Reds
30 December Ekaterinoslav falls to the Reds

1920 **3 January** Tsaritsyn falls to the Reds
4 January Kolchak abdicates
5–8 January Taganrog, Novocherkassk and Rostov-on-Don fall to the Reds
2 February Estonia and Bolsheviks sign peace treaty
7 February Kolchak executed in Irkutsk
7 February Odessa falls to the Reds
19 February White Northern Government falls, Archangel
17 March Red Army takes Ekaterinodar
27 March Reds enter Novorossisk
1 April Americans evacuate Siberia
4 April Denikin resigns, Wrangel assumes command

The cruiser *Aurora*, whose guns heralded the arrival of Bolshevism. (Sovietsky Kudoshnik, 1967)

6 April Far Eastern Republic established
24 April Russo-Polish War begins
27 April Red Army takes Azerbaijan
6 May Kiev falls to Poland
6 June Wrangel advances into the Tauride
12 June Kiev falls to the Reds
11 July Minsk falls to the Reds
14 July Vilna falls to the Reds
17 August Poland counter-attacks
19 August Antonov Rebellion begins in Tambov region
12 October Russo-Polish armistice
25 October Red offensive against Wrangel on the Dnieper Line
2 November Wrangel defends Crimea
11 November Perekop defences breached
14 November Wrangel evacuates Crimea
25 November Reds begin liquidation of the Makhnovshchina
December Red Army occupies Armenia

1921 **1921–23** Famine rages in Ukraine, Armenia, in the Crimea and along the Volga
1921–22 White resistance continues in Russian Far East and in parts of Central Asia
25 February Bolsheviks establish power in Georgia
2–18 March Kronstadt Rebellion crushed by the Red Army
2 April Bolsheviks establish power in Armenia
August Makhnovshchina crushed by the Red Army
15 September Execution of Roman von Ungern-Sternberg, the 'Mad Baron'

1922 **Spring** Antonov Rebellion crushed by the Red Army
25 October Japan evacuates Vladivostok
19 November Bolsheviks annex the Far Eastern Republic

Новороссійскъ - Novorossisk
Общій видъ.

1923 January–March Lieutenant-General Pepeliev invades Yakutsk with the Siberian Volunteer Corps and is defeated. Pepelyaev captured 17 June

The southern White port and Allied supply depot of Novorossisk on the Black Sea. From 1919, the British used this port to supply their military mission training Denikin's Whites in the arts of logistics, aircraft handling, tank-driving and gunnery.

The October Revolution

'It was with a sense of awe that they turned upon Russia the most grisly of all weapons. They transported Lenin in a sealed truck like a plague bacillus into Russia.'
– Winston Churchill, *The World Crisis*, Volume Five

The 304-year reign of the Romanov dynasty came to an end on 15 March 1917 (Gregorian calendar, new-style date). The Russian 'February Revolution' had begun in earnest on 8 March, much as the French Revolution of 1789 had, as a direct result of women marching in search of bread. For the first time in imperial history, military forces sent to quell the ever-widening circle of discontented citizens of Petrograd refused to fire and actually joined the demonstrators. The hard winter of 1917 had exacerbated the food and fuel shortages and had compounded the widespread discontent that had reached endemic proportions over Russia's ill-fated participation in World War One.

In the words of Vassily Shulgin, a conservative politician in the Duma, 'Only hot lead could drive this terrible beast, that somehow had burst free, back into its den.' But no hot lead was forthcoming. Out of an available garrison of 180,200 troops in the environs of Petrograd, 170,000 had taken to the streets. The order of Tsar Nicholas II to put an end 'to all disturbances in the capital' fell on deaf ears.

Crowds began tearing down images of the double-headed eagle, ancient symbol of the Romanovs. In vain, Nicholas sought to rally a favourable political consensus and bodies of still-loyal troops. However, one by one, his great captains and politicians recommended abdication, an action he undertook aboard his imperial train on 15 March.

This 'February Revolution' caught Russia's political exiles, including Bolshevik Party leader Vladimir Ilyich Ulyanov (alias Lenin), by surprise. Born in 1870, Lenin had by his teenage years become a devotee of Karl Marx, the German ideologue who had written the *Communist Manifesto* in 1848. His politically subversive writings led to his exile to Siberia from 1895 to 1900, after which he left Russia for Europe to travel, engage in political polemics and to study and lecture at the University of Zurich. Active in politics, Lenin led the Bolshevik faction of the Russian Social Democratic Labour Party from 1903, a faction fully committed to revolution.

Calculating that a dangerous revolutionary could help further undermine Russia's fragile commitment to continuing the war, the Germans assisted Lenin's travel from Switzerland across their territory to Finland. After crossing the Russo-Finnish border, Lenin arrived at Finland Station, Petrograd, on Easter Sunday 1917. There, in the darkened evening illuminated by spotlights, he delivered the first of his speeches on top of an armoured car, the famous 'April Theses' extolling continued revolution and hard action against the Provisional Government. Political factions that had been united in the fall of the tsar now emerged to each push their particular agenda to the fore. Leon Trotsky, the future architect of the Red Army, and Josef Stalin, the future dictator of the Soviet Union, had arrived earlier, Stalin from Siberia to take up his new post as Bolshevik Central Committee boss in Petrograd, and Trotsky from a recent trip to the United States.

Meanwhile, the new Provisional Government had formed in mid-March, a coalition of predominately middle-class, liberal-socialists. This government would be 'provisional' until full, representative elections could be held to determine the political composition of a Constituent

The origins of communism in Russia

The Russian Social Democratic Labour Party (RSDLP), which was committed to Marxist principles, formed in Minsk, Russia in March 1898. The party split in 1903–04, during the Second Party Congress in London, the faction led by Lenin insisting on a platform of 'democratic centralism', or a group of elite revolutionaries leading a limited party membership. The other side, led by Julius Martov, argued for a much larger party with significantly greater participation and wider democratic powers. This issue was critical because a larger membership would ensure a greater democratic process, but naturally be more divisive on the path to reform or revolution. A central party elite, on the other hand, could be more decisive, but practically lead to the concentration of power into too few hands.

Although neither faction normally had a majority in the proceedings, Lenin's supporters, by winning a narrow one-time vote, became known as Bolsheviks or 'majority' (socialists), while Martov's adherents received the less attractive accolade of Mensheviks or 'minority' (socialists). Attempts at collusion and compromise failed and in 1912, the Bolsheviks expelled the Mensheviks from the RSDLP and formed their own separate faction within the Duma in 1913, a faction that would accelerate the road to revolution.

In 1918, the party became known as the All-Union Communist Party (Bolsheviks). Under Lenin and the early years of Stalin, 'Bolshevik' and 'Communist' were often used interchangeably, although the foreign press, the Whites and the Nationalists tended to use 'Bolshevik'. During the period of Allied Intervention, British soldiers referred to them as 'Bolshies', the Americans calling them 'Bolos'. In 1952, at Stalin's behest it became the Communist Party of the Soviet Union and the word Bolshevik became *passé*, relegated to the early period of development and the civil war.

The Gates of the Winter Palace, stormed by the Red Guards during the October Revolution. These gates were immortalized in the Sergei Eisenstein film *October* in the 1920s. (Bullock collection)

Assembly, which would itself decide the future government of Russia. Prince Georgi Lvov, a liberal member of the Duma, proved acceptable as the first prime minister, while Alexander Kerensky, a Socialist Revolutionary, became first minister of justice.

In the turbulent months ahead, Kerensky's career enjoyed a meteoric rise: he became minister for war on 18 May and prime minister on 21 July. These roles brought him into direct confrontation with Lenin. Lenin's message of 'Peace, Land and Bread' was particularly challenging to Kerensky's coalition. 'Peace' meant surrendering to the aspirations of the Central Powers and an abrogation of pledges Russia had given to the Allies. 'Land', the Socialist Revolutionaries were prepared to give, and the Liberals willing to discuss, but only after the future Constituent Assembly had elected a new Duma and had hammered out the details constitutionally. 'Bread' would be a problem that not even the Bolshevik Revolution could solve.

Ironically, both Kerensky and Lenin had several personal circumstances in common: Kerensky hailed from the same town as Lenin – Simbirsk on the Volga – both had Jewish blood and both had studied law at university. Kerensky's father, in fact, had briefly taught the young Lenin.

Nevertheless, increasingly two governments existed side-by-side in the capital: the ever-shifting coalitions of the Provisional Government and the more

Alexander Kerensky (right). (Museum of Contemporary Events in Russia, 1926)

shadowy but vociferous government of the Petrograd Soviet of Workers' Deputies, composed of Socialist Revolutionaries, Mensheviks and Bolsheviks who leaned towards Lenin rather than Kerensky.

Remaining committed to the war, the Provisional Government undertook the 'July Offensive' in support of the Allies who were deadlocked with the Central Powers on the Western Front. After initial successes, the offensive became costly and in several sectors the ensuing retreat assumed the proportions of a rout. Seizing on the resulting demonstrations against the war and agitation for land reform, the Bolsheviks attempted to overthrow the Provisional Government from 16 to 18 July, an abortive coup known as the 'July Days'. Lenin, whom Kerensky had ordered to be shot on sight, went into hiding while Trotsky was arrested.

On 1 August, Kerensky appointed General Lavr Kornilov commander-in-chief, an appointment he would soon regret. Driven by the need to restore order at the front, Kornilov moved against the Provisional Government from 6 to 14 September, ordering General Krymov's 3rd Cavalry Corps to capture Petrograd. Kornilov's stated purpose was to purge the city and government of disloyal elements and save Russia.

In response, Kerensky opened the arsenals to arm the Petrograd Soviet who promptly called on all loyal adherents to erect field emplacements at key points controlling the city. Deputations of agitators met Krymov's troops en route, and through fraternization so demoralized them that the advance melted away. Thoroughly shaken, Krymov committed suicide. Kornilov was arrested along with the generals that had supported him, including Denikin, Lukomsky, Romanovsky and Markov.

While Lenin hid out in a small peasant's hut in the woods north of the capital, Kerensky took up quarters in the former tsar's imperial suite at the Winter Palace, each waiting for the final struggle. Meanwhile, soviets, or 'councils', sprang to power in Russia's towns and cities. Nationalists, inspired by the devolution of authority away from the geographical centre, began preparations to declare autonomy or independence from the former Russian Empire.

By early October, the Bolsheviks had managed to win a majority in the Petrograd Soviet and Trotsky was elected chairman on the 6th. Lenin arrived surreptitiously in Petrograd the following day, and on the 13th began demanding an immediate uprising against the government, an exhortation that was agreed to during a meeting of the Congress of Soviets of the Northern Region three days later. Forty thousand men of the Latvian Rifles, former tsarist soldiers who had been converted to Bolshevism, were promised to counter any move by Kerensky. The Military Revolutionary Committee was formed on 25 October, and the Bolsheviks established their main position at the Smolny Institute in Petrograd where they could easily attack government facilities.

All eyewitnesses attest to the eerie, inexplicable calm that enveloped the city in the final days before the coup. Kerensky had surrounded his quarters at the Winter Palace with 800 troops, six armoured cars, six pieces of artillery and 19 machine guns. Both he and the commandant of the Petrograd garrison, Colonel Polkovnikov, expressed confidence that they were more than a match for the Bolsheviks. Not content to wait, on 5 November Kerensky ordered the arrest of the Military Revolutionary Committee, closed Bolshevik newspapers and cut the telephone lines to Smolny. Additional troops thought loyal were brought in, including the 1st Petrograd Women's Battalion. Visible tension had now come to the city.

On Tuesday, 6 November, the Bolsheviks strengthened Smolny with barricades and artillery. Both sides began taking control of key points in the city, including the bridges. Kerensky called a session of his ministers, but nothing except scuffles in the street had taken place by evening. Lenin, waiting at a colleague's apartment, now penned a furious letter to the regional party committees, going directly to the membership, demanding immediate action. The letter ended with 'The Government is tottering. We must deal it the death blow at any cost.' He then moved directly to Smolny.

Kerensky meanwhile had been up all night. He positioned himself in the early hours of 7 November at the General Staff Building across the square from the Winter Palace where he issued orders to troops, who did not respond. Returning to the palace he took a moment's respite on the bed of Nicholas II before rising at 9 am to discover his phone connections dead and the closest bridge over the Neva River in Bolshevik hands.

The revolution that day assumed more of the proportions of a tragi-comedy than the blazing epic portrayed in later years by Soviet movie propagandist Sergei Eisenstein.[*] That morning, Kerensky decided to leave the city in order to raise loyal troops in person. This was not easy because Bolshevik sympathizers had disabled all Russian automobiles in the vicinity. Eventually, he convinced the American embassy to loan him a Renault car, which he said he would return in a few days. In the meantime, his staff also had commandeered a Pierce-Arrow car. Sitting in the Pierce-Arrow with the Renault in front, still flying the American flag from the hood, Kerensky raced off for the town of Gatchina and lunch.

Lenin also had been up most of the night. Wednesday, 7 November found him at Smolny with the Military Revolutionary Committee, demanding the coup go forward. At 10 am, he declared the deposition of the Provisional Government and Bolsheviks began plastering the announcement across the city. The government, however, still existed.

Throughout the day, Red Guards and sailors from Kronstadt gradually infiltrated the city and captured most strategic points in the central area. Entering the Mariinsky Palace that afternoon, they simply told the

---

[*] The revolutionary Soviet Russian film director whose four main films were *October*, *Battleship Potemkin*, *Alexander Nevsky* and *Ivan the Terrible*.

The Fortress of Peter and Paul. (© Corbis)

government officials to leave, and they did. By late afternoon all communications centres, railway terminals and major public buildings were in their hands. The garrison of Petrograd had stood idly by, refusing to take sides.

Meanwhile, the last of Kerensky's ministers had retreated to the Malachite Chamber of the Winter Palace to await events. Their defenders were a handful of cadets and the 1st Petrograd Women's Battalion, much of the other garrison having trickled away in sections. Upon this tiny group the Bolsheviks now focused their attention. According to convention, the defenders would be asked to surrender, and if they did not, a red lantern would be hoisted and the cruiser *Aurora*, anchored nearby, would commence firing on the Winter Palace.

In the end, the ultimatum was refused and the Bolsheviks, failing to find a red lantern, eventually shot off a purple flare. This was thought good enough and the *Aurora* started firing at 6:30 pm, but only with blank shells. Orders to have the guns at the Fortress of Peter and Paul start firing were to no avail

because those guns had not been properly serviced. Eventually, at 11 pm, these were brought into line but 33 of the shells fell wide, only two hitting and damaging the plaster of inside rooms. In response, the cadets fired their machine guns into the dark and the Women's Battalion got up and left.

The last moments came at 2 am on 8 November when the Bolsheviks, who had already infiltrated the palace in force, prepared to enter the room where the remnants of Kerensky's ministers resided. One faithful cadet prepared to make the last stand, but the minister of justice declined to countenance violence. Military Revolutionary Committee member Vladimir Antonov-Ovseenko walked through the door at the head of his Bolshevik troops and announced the arrest of the Provisional Government.

Such was the vaunted October Revolution. Only six casualties resulted and these among the attackers. In Lenin's own words, the Party had 'found power lying in the streets and simply picked it up'.

As news of the revolution's success in Petrograd spread, similar uprisings occurred in most of Russia's cities. At noon on 7 November, the Bolsheviks in Moscow began forming a Military Revolutionary Committee while the mayor of the city, a Socialist Revolutionary, began organizing a Committee of Public Safety, both sides girding for conflict.

Fifty thousand Red Guards, most hailing from the city's many factories, invaded the city centre and captured the ancient medieval fortress, the Kremlin. In response, on 9 November, the Committee of Public Safety directed its 10,000 men, consisting of officers, cadets and the still-dependable troops at its disposal to counter-attack. They recaptured the city centre, with the Kremlin falling the following day.

Over the next few days, Moscow's defenders held the city centre in street-to-street fighting while Lenin ordered reinforcements and arms into the city from outlying areas in support of the Reds. On 15 November the Kremlin was breached by

Lenin (centre) and Stalin (centre right) hear the opening guns of the cruiser *Aurora*. (Painting, by S. I. Dudnik, c. 1930s)

artillery and the final Red Guard assault went in. The Bolsheviks suffered 228 killed, while the number of dead among the defenders went unrecorded.

As the new Bolshevik-dominated regime came to power, the struggle to retain that power began in earnest. On 13 November, the Petrograd Red Guards had successfully turned back General Krasnov's Cossacks at Pulkovo Heights, just outside the city. This ended the threat of Kerensky's counter-revolution. However, Russia was still technically at war with the Central Powers. Moreover, new nationalist states based on the peripheries of the now-broken empire began to declare independence: the Ukraine on 20 November, Finland on 6 December, and Lithuania, Latvia and Estonia in the early weeks of 1918.

Russia was in chaos. Industrial production had come to a standstill. Winter was coming and the scarcity of food in the hungry cities promised famine. Ominously, those discontented with the path of revolution began to gather. And Russia would soon be plunged into the bloodiest civil war of the 20th century.

'Storming the Winter Palace' by P. P. Sokolov-Skalia. (Iskusstvo, 1940)

An Empire Divided

The Whites

Contrary to Soviet propaganda, most of the Whites were not monarchists. They had lived through the fall of the tsar in March 1917 and the assassination of the royal family in July 1918. Indeed, General Mikhail Alexiev had advised the tsar to abdicate in 1917 and General Lavr Kornilov had actually arrested the tsarina. Both men would become prominent leaders of the White movement later that year. Nevertheless, most of the Whites had felt comfortable enough under the tsar's regime.

Officers and politicians who remained pro-monarchist attached themselves to each of the White armies because politically there was nowhere else for them to turn. Tension would surface in each of the White armies between those favouring the more democratic progressivism of the February Revolution and those who could not reconcile themselves to it. They made a common if uneasy cause against the Bolsheviks.

From November 1917 through the spring of 1918 and even beyond, those who would fight the civil war began to choose sides. Overall, the White armies were middle class in orientation but were amazingly heterogeneous. Their ranks contained the full spectrum of former Russian society, from peasant to noble. They were united only through their opposition to Bolshevism, a political movement that they regarded as anti-religious, anti-property, anti-business and anti-Russian.

Consequently, the Whites failed to promulgate a comprehensive and coherent political platform upon which all, or even most, could enthusiastically agree. Each of the White factions, from the Southern Front under Generals Denikin and Wrangel, to the Northwestern Front under General Yudenich,

to the Northern Front under General Miller, to the Siberian Front under Admiral Kolchak, published manifestos calling for the political formation of a future Constituent Assembly that would operate according to European-style parliamentarian procedures. Officially, each of the White factions eschewed engaging in politics until victorious and a Constituent Assembly could be convened in Moscow to decide Russia's future.

This stance cost them the support of a wider social base, particularly over the question of land reform. Russia remained an overwhelmingly rural and agricultural nation in the early 20th century. The nobility, the state church and the *nouveaux riches* collectively possessed too much of the arable land. The immediate question, much as in the earlier French Revolution, was whether to recognize the revolutionary seizures of land and property that had been carried out at the grassroots level in 1917 and which had been largely sanctioned by Kerensky's Provisional Government.

The primary White leaders, General Anton Ivanovich Denikin, General Petr Nikolayevich Wrangel and Admiral Alexander Kolchak, tried to institute land reform but most lacked either the political expertise or the best advisors to implement their policies. Wrangel suffered defeat before his more enlightened policies could take effect. Too often, the old landlords followed in the wake of the White armies, attempting to turn back the clock to 1916 and repossess the lands they had lost.

Also costly was the determination of the Whites to honour Russia's commitment to the Allies in World War One, a resolve that would last until Armistice Day, 11 November 1918. Given Russia's general exhaustion, continuing the war was exceedingly unpopular with the general population.

Russian troops charging with a regimental flag bearing a religious image. Such a scene was typical of the White armies on all fronts. (Russian painting, 1910s)

Nevertheless, most of the Whites chose to place their faith in the Allies. Logically, after winning the war, the Allies would then help the Whites defeat Bolshevism. They sincerely believed the Bolsheviks were the hirelings of imperial Germany and their evidence seemed conclusive: Lenin had been exported to Russia by the Germans and many of the early Red Guard units they faced were heavily permeated with former German and Austro-Hungarian prisoners of war.

All White factions were loath to recognize the independence of the many new states that had broken away from the former Russian

Empire in 1917–18. These included Estonia, Latvia, Lithuania, Belarus, Poland, Ukraine and the Caucasian states. Denikin coined the phrase 'Russia One and Indivisible', a phrase that resonated with each of the other White leaders, and an ideal meant to keep 'Mother Russia' intact. This ideal alienated the new nationalistic states that had no intention of surrendering their ethnicity, language and independence and returning to the Russian fold. Failure to recognize reality and the aspirations of the breakaway nations cost the Whites critical support against the Bolsheviks to whom the new states themselves were generally opposed.

Above all, the Whites were military men rather than politicians. On each front, they elevated a general and vested him with wide civil and military powers, thinking that this man would create unity and lead them to victory, and that the Russian people would later decide, through the electoral process, what form of government was best. To those who did not readily understand this point of view, and more still to their opponents, the White approach appeared as a veiled dictatorship.

White ideology may be seen in the representative symbols they chose to adopt. Propaganda posters portrayed the Bolsheviks as destroyers, red with blood, gloating over the remains of the Russian Empire. Their flags, from the highest level down to battalion markers, often depicted saints, Orthodox or Maltese crosses, references to God, and expressions or images of patriotism and unity for the homeland. Many shock units carried banners with the skull and crossbones, implying readiness for sacrifice and death.

The early Whites on all fronts were volunteers almost to a man. Heavily outnumbered, they survived through an intense commitment to their cause and by sheer military prowess. By autumn 1918, however, heavy losses in the field caused them to resort to conscription from the newly-won territories. This resulted in a certain weakening of their units overall, even as the number of units in their order

of battle increased. More dubious was the adoption of former Red soldiers into their own ranks, a method of recruitment that accelerated throughout 1919. Some former Red veterans, given retraining and a new cause, fought extremely well while others sought the first opportunity to desert.

Foreign observers noted the large number of young soldiers in the White armies. The Whites and their Cossack allies hesitated to conscript classes of soldiers that had been infected by extreme socialism in World War One, the so-called *frontoviki*. They turned instead to young men, even boys, from Russia's many military schools, the cadets and junkers, who fought gallantly for their cause. Most White units also had a disproportionate number of officers and there were cases of senior officers serving in the ranks as privates. Many battalions had an 'officer's company' which formed an elite on the battlefield and could supply critical

Russian officer in 1917 displaying the white flower of loyalty and honour. Many such young and idealistic men fought heroically in the White armies. (Bullock collection)

cadres to rebuild destroyed units or provide officers for newly-formed units.

Although largely proficient as infantry and in the technical arms, the Whites relied on the Cossacks to furnish the majority of their cavalry. Most numerous in the south were the Don Cossacks, followed, respectively, by the Kuban, Terek and Astrakhan hosts. In the east, the Orenburg, Ural and Siberian Cossacks supported the Whites on the front lines, while the hosts of the Semirechie, Amur, Ussuri and Trans-Baikal protected the lines of communication and often pursued semi-independent policies.

Each Cossack host attempted to preserve their ancient traditions, privileges and way of life during the course of the civil war. These had been eroded under the tsars from the 18th century through a policy of 'Russification', and further diluted by the presence of a growing number of *inogorodnye* or 'outsiders' living in Cossack lands. In the case of the Don and Kuban, these outsiders represented approximately half of the population. The Cossacks traditionally had been mounted soldiers who received plots of land and a measure of local autonomy in exchange for military service. The average Cossack was proud, protective of his culture and Orthodox in religion. In time, each Cossack *voisko* (military host or army) correctly came to see the Bolsheviks as inimical to their way of life.

The Reds, the Blacks, the Greens

The Reds themselves were heterogeneous, especially in the first year of the civil war. From 1917 to 1918, the Red Army was a collection of revolutionary factions which included the Bolsheviks, Mensheviks, Left Socialist Revolutionaries, Right Socialist Revolutionaries, the Jewish Bund, Anarchists, various smaller agrarian peasant and 'social democratic' parties, and even groups known as the 'Greens'. The Whites made little or no distinction between these elements and referred to them simply as 'Reds'.

The Bolsheviks in fact considered themselves to be the only 'valid' Reds. Consequently, step-by-step, they began to suppress all factions that did not fully support their own points of view, a process complete by 1922. Unlike the Whites, who generally acted honourably if inflexibly, the Bolshevik leadership had no scruples about forming temporary alliances against a common enemy then liquidating that former ally in turn.

The term 'Bolshevik' actually meant 'majority (socialist)' while 'Menshevik' meant 'minority (socialist)'. Prior to 1903, both the Bolsheviks and Mensheviks had belonged to the Marxist Russian Social Democratic Labour Party (RSDLP). Both believed in leadership by an elite core of professional revolutionaries, but whereas the Mensheviks supported wider participation by party members and cooperation with the existing government, the Bolsheviks determined to limit party membership and to attack the government from without. Irreconcilable differences continued until the final split in 1912, after which the Bolsheviks carried the RSDLP moniker alone. After using the Mensheviks for their own purposes during the civil war, the Bolsheviks outlawed them in 1921.

The Socialist Revolutionaries (SRs) were another matter. Russia was a predominately agrarian country and the SRs were committed to a platform that addressed the needs of the peasants in contradistinction to the Bolsheviks who supported the industrial proletariat, who, they believed, would lead world revolution. A critical issue was the distribution of land. While the SRs believed that land should be socialized, or divided up among the working peasantry, the Bolsheviks pushed for the nationalization of land, a concept eventually leading to the state-operated communal farms.

Immensely popular among the peasantry, the SRs formed the largest political bloc in 1917. In the pre-Constituent Assembly elections of 12 November 1917, elections intended to select delegates to the assembly scheduled for January 1918, the SRs polled 57 per cent, with the Bolsheviks a distant second at 25 per cent. However, the SRs were split internally. From summer 1917, the (Left) SRs had frequently supported the Bolsheviks, especially over the issues of ousting the Provisional Government by coup and immediately confiscating and redistributing land from the landowners to the peasants.

Lenin himself had determined to overturn the results of the pre-Constituent Assembly elections held in November, elections that he had lost. As delegates to the official meeting of the Constituent Assembly prepared to take their seats in the Tauride Palace in Petrograd on 19 January 1918, they found themselves locked out and turned away by Bolshevik armed guards. Lenin announced the dissolution of the Constituent Assembly that same day.

The mainstream SRs, generally known outside their party as (Right) SRs, now had to choose between Whites and Reds, or find, in the words of their leader, Viktor Chernov, a 'third way'. Consequently, Right SR leaders moved to Samara on the Volga in June where they formed the Committee of Members of the Constituent Assembly or KOMUCH. Immediately they began to raise anti-Bolshevik military units which, nevertheless, hoisted a red flag. As a result, many of the more conservative White politicians and soldiers in Siberia and on the Volga unfairly dismissed them as Reds.

The Left SRs also found themselves in opposition to the Bolsheviks after Lenin and Trotsky blessed the signing of the Treaty of Brest-Litovsk in March 1918 to conclude Russia's participation in World War One, a treaty that dismembered large portions of Russia and imposed a punitive peace. Thereafter, many Left SRs decided to cooperate with the Allies and reform an Eastern Front against the Central Powers.

Coordinating a revolt with Allied intelligence agents and in response to the Allied landings in Siberia and North Russia which occurred that spring and summer, the Left SRs rose in revolt against the Bolsheviks in Moscow and at Yaroslavl in July, and after days of street fighting were slaughtered by the Cheka and the elite Latvian Rifles. Survivors of the SR Party in general who had not accommodated themselves to the Bolsheviks by the end of the civil war were sentenced to death in 1922.

The Reds also contained in their ranks many Anarchists who were often characterized by themselves and their enemies as 'Black Guards', black representing the colour of negation, the removal of state authority. The Anarchists were a genuine grassroots movement believing in local autonomy and freely elected 'soviets', or councils, and therefore chafed under the increasing bureaucracy and centralism Bolshevism came to represent. They believed in the revolutionary seizure of land and its redistribution to those who would till the land, but they were hostile to the communal, state-controlled farms espoused by the Bolsheviks.

Some Anarchists chose to work with the Bolsheviks, hoping for a moderation of their policies, and managed to maintain an affiliation until the end of the civil war. Others, like Nestor Makhno, variously allied with the Bolsheviks or fought them in the field. Many Anarchists were purged during and after the crackdown on Anarchist centres in Moscow in April 1918, after the Kronstadt rebellion in March 1921 and during the Bolshevik liquidation of Makhno's movement that same year.[*]

The Greens were another a diverse group who allied themselves with the Reds when it suited their purposes and fought them when it did not. The Greens ranged from nationalists who sought independence for their particular region, to outcast SRs or Anarchists, to simple bandits. Some were highly committed to a political platform linked to land ownership and local rule,

---

[*] The Kronstandt Rebellion of 1921 was an attempt by the sailors of the Baltic Fleet to ensure that the Bolshevik Party adhered to the original principles of the revolution, such as the rights to free assembly and the establishment of trade unions. However, the rebellion was ruthlessly crushed.

'Brothers' by P. P. Sokolov-Skalia. The brother (right) is either in the White Army or has not yet joined the Reds, much to the indignation of his Red brother at left. (Iskusstvo, 1940)

as in the violent Antonov Rebellion of 1920–22, while others were merely hiding out from military conscription, whether Red or White.

Some Greens called themselves 'Forest Brethren', and lived in the deep woods or *taiga* with an almost piratical code of life and honour. Soviet historians estimated that of the 100,000 or more Red partisans operating against Kolchak's White Siberians in 1919–20, probably over half were actually Greens in orientation. Characteristically, the Red Army brought the Greens to heel at the end of the civil war, although survivors managed to resist in Siberia and Central Asia well into the 1920s.

The Red Army, therefore, was a coalition of factions content to fight the Whites, and then each other when the Whites were no longer a threat. As the civil war progressed, the Red Army became more homogenous, more Bolshevik in nature.

From the start of the Revolution, the Bolsheviks possessed several key advantages over their opponents. Consolidating a revolution is never easy, and for that reason the great majority throughout history have failed. Extraordinary leadership is essential, leadership that includes an abundance of grey matter, clarity of vision, the ability to adapt ideology, if only temporarily, along a more pragmatic, even unscrupulous path, and an iron ruthlessness to sacrifice – and to making others sacrifice – for the end goal.

These things the predominately middle-class, professional-revolutionary Bolshevik leadership possessed. Irrevocably committed to destroying one world and building another, they had the almost astounding arrogance to create that which had not been created before, a world that only existed as a theory, thoughtfully formulated on paper while in exile, or feverishly composed in the mind while running from the tsarist secret police.

Equally important in their first year, they had won the support of three key military forces that would allow them to dominate any one opponent in a given time and place. These were the armed sailors of the Baltic Fleet, the elite Latvian Rifle Division and the dedicated 'proletarian' workers who made up the majority of the paramilitary Red Guard.

'Red Partisans in Ambush' by A. Nikulin. Partisans came in various political colours – Red, White, Black (Anarchist), and Green (non-affiliated guerrillas or 'Forest Brethren'). Many partisan bands maintained loyalty only to themselves or to their particular creed, supporting neither Red nor White. They constituted 'The Third Force', making and breaking temporary alliances, menacing rear areas, and even engaging in pitched battles against smaller units. (Art card, Museum of the Revolution, 1928)

Moreover, the Bolsheviks were ensconced in Moscow, Petrograd and central Russia, where the many arms factories and stores of weapons that had supported the country's campaigns in World War One lay. Additionally, central Russia was comparatively rich in railways. These facts allowed the Bolsheviks to equip their military forces and deploy them where needed.

The Bolsheviks expanded the Red Army during the course of the civil war. The sailors, given their greater technical skills, provided experienced cadres for the artillery, armoured car and armoured trains units. Conscription raised large numbers of Russia's peasantry, who along with the Red Guard units provided the backbone of the infantry. As for cavalry, the Bolsheviks largely employed the *inogorodnye* who lived on Cossack lands and who were familiar with horses but were not themselves Cossack.

The Reds, like the Whites, utilized symbols representative of their movement.

To the people who endured the civil war, the political colours of Red, White, Green and Black were often secondary to sheer survival. (Bullock collection)

For centuries, the colour red had suggested revolution, but it had also been the favourite colour of the tsars. From the red facings of St Basil's Cathedral in Moscow to Red Square itself, to the fortunate double meaning of the word *krasnaia* – which can mean either 'red' or 'beautiful' – the Bolsheviks were able to hijack the colour red for their own purposes.

Red armbands with black letters indicating the particular military unit were worn by the Red Guards. Red metal stars adorned *furashki* (caps) while cloth stars appeared on the uniforms of 1919 and 1922. Red stars on military equipment or political placards suggested a new future, especially when linked with the red and golden rays of dawn. The golden hammer and plough placed on red flags and billboards linked the new movement with progressive changes on behalf of the industrial proletariat and peasant.

Overall the Bolshevik message, whether direct or subliminal, was simple and easily understood by Russia's illiterate: peace, land and bread. The slogan 'All Power to the Soviets' – the soviet supposedly being a 'democratic' council in which the worker or peasant received representation and justice – appealed to those who did not yet understand what Bolshevism and the new soviets were all about. These and other slogans were painted in suggestive collages, and in narrative, almost comic-book scenes, in the new artistic style known as *avant garde*. This art appeared throughout the Red heartland on town posters and on the sides of special agitation-propaganda trains and riverboats.

Symbols were also designed to replace political authority in the minds of the people. Depictions of Lenin appeared everywhere, especially in places where images of the tsar had been. Those unable to comprehend Bolshevism nevertheless ascertained, if only by suggestion, that there was a new figure of power, a new Red Tsar.

1918

Red consolidation

The Russian Soviet Federated Socialist Republic (RSFSR) came into being on 7 November 1917, the day of the Revolution, the constitution of the new state being ratified on 7 July 1918. One of the first acts of state was to change the capital, previously at Petrograd, to Moscow on 10 March 1918.

The Bolsheviks faced many critical challenges in their first year: how to consolidate their base and preserve their power, how to improve the economy and feed the people, how to respond to external challenges from the Germans, and those of the counter-revolutionaries (Whites, Anarchists, non-compliant Socialist Revolutionaries, and eventually the Allies), how to create a new army, and how to centralize and impose an iron discipline on that army and society itself. These were the problems that make revolutions fail.

The Bolshevik Revolution had been carried out under the slogan 'All Power to the Soviets'. This did not mean 'Power to the Bolsheviks' because Lenin's party was only one in the wider political spectrum. Nor did the term 'soviets' mean 'communists', as many in the West loosely applied it later during the Cold War. The soviets were workers' and soldiers' councils, some 900 of which had sprung up throughout the cities, factories and Red Guard units of the former Russian Empire during the upheavals of 1917.

These had elected delegates to the All Russian Congress of Soviets, the political entity in the name of which the Revolution had taken place. The standing body of this Congress was the Central Committee (later the Politburo) headed by Lenin and including Trotsky, Sverdlov and Stalin. The Soviet or Council of People's Commissars, known as *Sovnarkom*, acted as a cabinet of professionals who were assigned specific portfolios. Other departments, committees and positions, such as the Central Committee of the Bolshevik Party and the General Secretary, pertained exclusively to the dominant Bolshevik Party itself.

The soviets proved to be an important means of Bolshevik political consolidation. Each soviet echelon, from highest to lowest, elected a Military Revolutionary Committee, an arm empowered to 'take action' on behalf of the host soviet. The factories, army units and larger cities tended to be dominated by the Bolshevik Party, a fact that gave Lenin an almost decisive advantage over his political opponents. In a word, the Bolsheviks had 'troops', namely the revolutionized urban proletariat and factory workers, and the soldiers and sailors known as Red Guards. Beyond these, the Bolsheviks had the assured support of the elite Latvian Division, a 'revolutionized' body of at least 18,000 men divided into ten regiments. Moreover, increasing control of the soviets, or at least the more critical ones, gave Lenin a loose command-and-control structure throughout Russia. As a result, all political rivals, from the Socialist Revolutionaries to the Anarchists and the Mensheviks, had been effectively neutralized by late spring 1918.

Given control of the cities and railways, the Bolsheviks could easily wield power in the countryside. Lenin further extended this power into the rural areas through his promotion of the 'Committees of Village Poor', or *Kombedy*. The Bolsheviks promoted the destabilization of the countryside by setting the poorer peasants against the so-called 'middle peasants' who had slightly better living conditions, and especially against the hated *kulaks* or richer peasants. The *Kombedy* were encouraged, with Bolshevik blessing, to seize the holdings

The ancient medieval fortress of the Kremlin. It was to be the Bolsheviks' new seat of power, and Moscow their new capital. (© Corbis)

of richer peasants and if necessary through cooperative action with the Red Guards. The profits were divided between the poorer peasants and the supporters of Bolshevism residing in the urban areas.

These actions went hand-in-hand with the policy known as 'loot the looters' taking place simultaneously in the towns and cities. Supporters of the Revolution were encouraged to take over all industrial enterprises, seize church property and local banks and take the possessions of the nobility and the middle classes or bourgeoisie. These were cunning policies that won the Bolsheviks support from the poorer elements of society, whether urban or rural, and arguably established a grassroots base that would either actively promote, or at least acquiesce in, future Party actions. Official

nationalization of property and the means of production began under the auspices of the Supreme Council of the National Economy in mid-1918.

The Bolsheviks, who had been instrumental in destroying the morale of the army of the Provisional Government through agitation and propaganda, now had to build a new army capable of taking the field. For a month after the Revolution, the Russian Army had been left primarily to its own devices. Then, in December, the Bolsheviks issued an official schedule for phased demobilization. At the same time, carefully selected units were inducted into military formations that might be found useful in the future.

The infamous Order No. 1 issued in the spring of 1917 by the Provisional Government had abolished the death penalty, even for dereliction of duty or cowardice (although re-instituted by

Russia spring–autumn 1918

1. German intervention forces land in Finland, April 3.
2. Allied intervention forces start to arrive in Murmansk, April 5.
3. German intervention force in Georgia, May.
4. Czech Legion revolt, May 25.
5. Socialist Revolutionaries revolt at Yaroslavl and is crushed July 21.
6. Allied intervention forces arrive in Archangel, August 3.
7. British intervention forces arrive in Baku, August 4.
8. Izhevsk-Votkinsk Revolt, August.
9. French and Greek intervention forces arrive in Odessa-Kherson, December 17.

A   Turkish Occupation forces, 1917–18
B   Mannerheim's White Finns
C   Hetman Skoropadsky's Ukranians
D   Ataman Krasnov's Cossacks
E   Denkin's Volunteer Army

Central Powers area of occupation
Red Army area of occupation
Central Powers line of occupation
Volga Front
Junction of Donbas industrial towns

0   250 miles
0   500km

Kerensky in July, then overturned again by the SRs in November, then officially reinstated by the Bolsheviks in June 1918). Soldiers' councils, essentially mirror-images of the political councils or soviets, had been established throughout the Russian Army that same spring. These talked and tried to reach a consensus about military matters and

Vladimir Ilyich Ulyanov, 'Lenin', in Red Square,
25 May 1919. (Photo card, Planeta, 1969)

even strategy. Votes determined a particular
course of action.

These conditions lasted through the first
half of 1918. One White veteran, who had
spent several months in the Red Army before
he could defect to Denikin, confided to the
author that the majority of Red troops in
1918 were 'rubbish'. White memoirs based
on the interrogation of Red prisoners on the
Southern Front described the soldiers voting
on whether or not to defend a position,
whether to serve beyond one 'shift' of duty a
day or whether to work beyond the normal
hours of a working week. Positions were
sometimes left vacant because the occupants
were asleep or drinking. The Reds survived
these months for the simple reason that
their opponents were even weaker.

One problem in creating a revolutionary
army can be found in Bolshevik theory.
Officers, discipline, saluting and orders were
part of imperial 'class' traditions and were seen
as the trappings of nationalist-capitalist states.
The Revolution would be international in
scope, embracing the proletariat of all nations.
Volunteerism, spontaneity, duty to class
interests and revolutionary *élan* would
overcome the older and now irrelevant

methods of war. Once the Red Army came
into substantial contact with an imperialist
'oppressor' army, the soldiers of the latter
would find common solidarity with the
Bolsheviks and naturally desert. Field combat
against the Germans and Denikin's Volunteer
Army in the spring of 1918 sorely disabused
many of the Bolshevik leaders of these notions.

Another problem was how to convert
the Red Guards into more regular troops,
i.e. into what would become known as the
Red Army. The term 'Red Guards' has been
used interchangeably with 'Red', 'Red Army',
or forces of Reds. Specifically, however, 'Red
Guards' referred to 'politically conscious',
paramilitary formations that defended
revolutionary interests. By spring–summer
of 1917, Red Guards had formed in many of
Russia's cities as the militant arm of the soviets.

Red Guard units consisted of the 13-man
'decad' at the lowest level, four of these
making a corporal's squad, three of these
squads a company, and three companies a
battalion. Combined with technical troops,
the battalion totalled 500–600 men, all
battalions within a specific area falling
under the purview of the district division.
Officers were elected. Lacking an immediate,
professional army, the Red Guards, being
augmented by sailors, 'revolutionized'
soldiers from the front and international
volunteers, fought the first months of 1918
on their own.

Innumerable volunteer formations, more
accurately described as partisan groups, also
aided the Reds in 1918. These were bands
eager to engage in revolutionary activity and
which had been raised by a particular leader,
ataman or chieftain. The Bolsheviks employed
these groups, which often operated alongside
Red Guard units and later the Red Army.
However, they were seldom trusted. One
example, the hard-fighting Red 'Wolf Pack',
led by a Baltic sailor, had to be sent to the civil
war in Finland in spring 1918 to get them out
of the way of more regular operations.

Foundations for a more regular army
were laid in January, but the first official
units of the Red Army did not appear until
23 February 1918. Other landmarks followed:

on 22 April a decree for 'universal military training', on 10 May the incorporation of the majority of Red Guard forces into the Red Army, and on 12 June the first conscription of five birth years of the population (1892–97). By December 1918, the Red Army possessed a ration strength of 600,000.

These units needed officers, and during the first half of 1918 higher posts in the army had to be filled by former non-commissioned officers and leaders of the Red Guard. While several performed creditably, the majority had limited expertise. Four-month training courses were established in spring 1918 to raise their level of professionalism. However, these accretions were not enough to staff the rapidly expanding Red Army.

Utilization of the military specialist was the answer to this dilemma, a concept was championed, and steered to success, by the extraordinary man who became the architect of the Red Army, Leon Trotsky. This involved mobilizing former officers of the Imperial Army and placing them in positions of responsibility, a concept considered highly dangerous by many of the revolutionary leaders. These specialists would advise on technical matters, which ranged from supply to artillery to aviation. Some commanded military units (of all sizes) in the field. Nearly 50,000 had been mobilized by the end of the civil war.

Leon Davidovich Bronstein, popularly known as Lev Trotsky, inspects the elite Latvian Rifle Division as People's Commissar of Army and Navy Affairs in 1918. At far left is the commander of the elite Latvian Rifles, Ioakim Vatsetis. The Latvians were critical for the survival of the Bolshevik regime that first year, putting down revolts of Anarchists and Socialist Revolutionaries in Yaroslavl and Moscow. Regiments of Latvians fought on every front throughout the civil war. (*The Great War: The Standard History of the World-Wide Conflict*, vol. XVIII, August 1919)

'Shchors' by P. P. Sokolov-Skalia. N. A. Shchors fought against the Germans and Skoropadsky in 1918, against Petliura in 1919, and was killed in August of that year fighting the Poles. (Iskusstvo, 1940)

Family members of a military specialist were registered, their lives and his being forfeit in case of betrayal or lacklustre performance. Even so, there were notable instances of defection to the Whites. On balance, however, this system, combined with an allotment of full and even extra rations, worked very well. Lenin, who never once visited the front and who possessed almost no military expertise, nevertheless appreciated the daring and pragmatism behind the plan and backed Trotsky to the hilt. Intended as a temporary measure, most of the military specialists were only phased out by the late 1920s.

A new position, the 'commissar', was created to watch over these military specialists and to instil political correctness throughout the entire command structure. Each unit commander, whether he led a

front, an army, a corps, a division, a regiment or even a company, would receive as his opposite at least one commissar. The commander and commissar were considered equals. The commander ruled over military matters while the commissar reigned over political questions, including the state of a unit's morale and its level of revolutionary fervour. This system, begun more loosely in 1917, had largely taken hold by August 1918.

Leon Trotsky was primarily responsible for the genesis and nourishment of the Red Army. Trotsky (real name, Lev Davidovich Bronstein) was born into a Jewish family in Yanovka, Ukraine, in 1879. 'Trotsky' became his pseudonym while he pursued revolutionary activity against the tsar. A former Menshevik, he joined the Bolshevik Party in August 1917 and became a member of the Bolshevik Central Committee the following month. In September 1917 he was elected deputy of the Petrograd Workers' and Soldiers' Soviet and participated directly in the Revolution, after which he received successive posts as Commissar for Foreign Affairs from November 1917 and Commissar for War from March 1918 in the newly-formed Supreme Military Council.

Possessing no military experience, he nevertheless demonstrated a genius for military organization and a penchant for fiery oratory. Trotsky willingly subordinated himself to Lenin, even though he was arguably Lenin's intellectual equal. Trotsky himself, although a Marxist since 1898, had undergone a politically evolutionary process. Durinng the 1903–04 Second Party Congress held in London, Trotsky had opposed Lenin's position over the need for a party elite that would control the destiny of Marxism, a concept known as 'democratic centralism'. From 1904 to 1917, after a brief flirtation with the Mensheviks, he became a 'non-factional' member committed to overall unity. Undergoing a change of heart over Lenin's earlier position, Trotsky converted to the Bolshevik variant of the RSDLP, the party Lenin controlled, at the end of summer 1917.

Despite occasional arguments with Lenin, he maintained his essential support over the following years, referring to Lenin in his memoirs as 'the most manly of men', while recognizing his 'unerring political instinct'. Happily for the Bolshevik cause, this respect was reciprocated. Good relations, on the other hand, were not established with the man who would eventually become Trotsky's nemesis, both during and after the civil war, Josef Stalin.

Stalin was born in Gori, Georgia, in 1879, the son of poor peasants, his given names being Josef Vissarionovich Dzhugashvili. His mother, who called him 'Soso', sent him to an Orthodox seminary in Tiflis where he could become a respectable priest and escape his abusive, alcoholic father. As a young man, however, he became interested in the idea of socialist revolution and engaged in clandestine activity in Tiflis and Baku. Adopting the pseudonym 'Koba', he went through the usual arrests, exiles and escapes that were so necessary later if one wished to become part of the Bolshevik elite.

In 1912 he assumed the alias 'Stalin', or 'man of steel', that he maintained for the rest of his life. Preferring to operate as a power figure behind the scenes, he became one of the guiding lights of the *Pravda* (Truth) newspaper in 1917 and personally helped Lenin escape capture in July. In August he was elected to the Central Committee and in November was appointed Commissar of Nationalities. Throughout the civil war he held numerous positions as a special Political Commissar to endangered fronts. Stalin opposed the more regularized army as well as the use of former imperial officers, positions that naturally set him against Trotsky.

Increased organization and discipline were also necessary in the political realm. The All-Russian Extraordinary Commission for Combating Counter-Revolution and Sabotage, known more popularly as the Cheka, had formed in December 1917. The first Cheka combat detachment of 1,000 troops supplemented the field agents in March 1918. This force consisted of infantry, cavalry, artillery, machine guns and a section of armoured cars. The Cheka

'The Red Guard' by K. Maximov. (Art card, Museum of the Revolution, 1928)

as a whole contained an unusually high percentage of 'internationalists', including Poles, Finns, Jews, Latvians and Chinese who habitually dressed in black leathers. Felix 'Iron Felix' Dzerzhinsky, a Pole who had dreamed of becoming a Catholic priest before spending much of his life in prison, in exile, or on the run from police, commanded all Cheka franchises. Their motto, 'Shield and Sword of the Revolution', described their purpose.

Over time, the Cheka proved itself an equal-opportunity employer dedicated to internal repression. A few ex-tsarist prison guards remained at their posts and former criminals who exhibited revolutionary fervour accepted new positions without discrimination. One black man, a communist-internationalist who went by the name 'Johnson', skinned his victims alive before murdering them in Odessa. One high-born female known as the 'Baroness' played the role of stool pigeon among the prisoners at the notorious Lubyanka No. 11 jail in Moscow. Nina Maslova, the nymphomaniac lover of a Cheka agent, plied her sexual charms in exchange for needed information. Still another female, a Hungarian known by the sobriquet 'Remover', personally executed

80 young men, each in a way suggesting sexual obsession. Nor was alcohol or drug addiction a bar to employment. Before gruelling assignments, the Cheka distributed extra rations of liquor to their operatives and turned a blind eye to cocaine, as long as dutiful service was not impaired.

Local Cheka establishments dotted across Russia and the Ukraine, in fact, were noted for particular specializations. A few examples only will suffice. At Kremenchug the clergy were impaled on stakes, hand-saws were driven through bones at Tsaritsyn, victims were scalped at Kharkov, and crucifixion or stoning was *de rigueur* at Ekaterinoslav. A few were noted for their artistry: at Orel in winter, humans were turned, progressively, into virtual statues of ice. At each locale, women prisoners could expect to be assaulted and raped by one or more of the guards.

In 1999 the author requested a private tour of one such Cheka torture and execution room in Samara, situated in the basement of the city's current historical museum. Even after 80 years the bullet-pocked walls and smears of dried blood were much in evidence. Asking the director 'who were these people, what were they supposed to have done?', he received the grave reply, 'These were the people of our city.'

The application of 'Red Terror' against the enemies of the revolution became an officially sanctioned policy just hours after the attempted assassination of Lenin on 30 August 1918. Fanya Kaplan, a female Socialist Revolutionary, had become disgruntled with the Bolsheviks after they had shut down the Consituent Assembly and once the Treaty of Brest-Litovsk had been signed, surrendering a significant amount of Russian soil to the Central Powers. Seemingly in collusion with certain Allied agents, including the renowned master spy, Sidney Reilly, Kaplan accosted Lenin after his speech at a factory in Moscow. Each of her three pistol shots struck home, one bullet striking Lenin in the jaw, one entering his left shoulder while the third passed harmlessly through his suit

coat. None, however, were fatal. Briskly interrogated, Kaplan assumed sole responsibility and was summarily executed on 3 September.

The Cheka assumed additional roles throughout the civil war: frontier control, transport and railway security, espionage, counter-espionage, the officially-sanctioned 'extermination of the bourgeoisie', and fielding a combat corps of troops to whatever sector needed reinforcement or political stiffening. Special agents even lured the famous counter-revolutionary spies Boris Savinkov and Sidney Reilly to their doom. Rising to a strength of 37,000 by January 1919, Cheka totals peaked at 261,000 in October 1921, or roughly 10 per cent of the armed forces. In the end, the Cheka establishment proved itself no less heinous and pervasive than Heinrich Himmler's future SS in Nazi Germany.

Militarily, the RSFSR found itself in a critical position in 1918. First and foremost were the intentions of the Germans and their Austro-Hungarian allies. At any time, the Germans could have marched on Petrograd or Moscow. Lenin, however, championed peace with Germany and staked his considerable reputation on the process.

Trotsky, as Commissar of Foreign Affairs, conducted negotiations for an armistice leading up to the Treaty of Brest-Litovsk in March 1918. When the Bolsheviks dragged their feet over particular clauses, the Germans marched deep into the Ukraine and the Crimea in February. Bolshevik political resistance collapsed in the face of resolve and they accepted the punitive peace that followed, a peace that separated Finland, the Baltic States, Poland, the Ukraine, the Crimea and parts of the Caucasus from the former Russian Empire. Given geopolitical and strategic realities, nothing else could have been done.

Fortunately for the Bolsheviks, the peace with Germany held. When the Allies began intervening in August, the Reds were able to stand up the Sixth Army against the invasion on the Northern Front and hold their positions throughout the civil war. Allied

intervention in Siberia ultimately became
a chimera, easily opposed by the loosely
federated partisan units in the east. When
the Germans began withdrawing from Russia
and the Ukraine after the armistice that ended
World War One in November, the Bolsheviks
were able to maintain 'screens' of troops all
along their Western Front. The emerging
nationalist states on their western frontier
were not in a position to become a serious
threat. This fact allowed the Reds to
concentrate forces against the counter-
revolutionary Whites who had begun to form
along their eastern and southern frontiers.

First resistance: the Volunteer Army

Three White generals were instrumental in
organizing the first resistance that led to civil
war in the aftermath of the Bolshevik
Revolution: Lavr Kornilov, Mikhail Alexiev
and Anton Denikin. Kornilov, the son of a
Cossack, had been born in Siberia in 1870.
A man of reckless courage and almost
magical charisma, he had been the first
Russian general to escape from an enemy
prisoner-of-war camp in World War One.
By 31 July 1917, he had risen to the position
of supreme commander-in-chief under
Kerensky. In August, in an attempt to restore
order at the front and continue the war
against the Central Powers, Kornilov
attempted to overturn the Provisional
Government and failed.

Alexiev, the son of a simple soldier,
had been born in 1857. Fighting in both
the Russo-Turkish War of 1877–78 and the
Russo-Japanese War of 1904–05, Alexiev
became a professor of military science before
serving as chief of staff when Tsar Nicholas II
assumed personal command of the Russian
Army in September 1915. He then became

commander-in-chief from March to June
1917, becoming chief of staff once more
under Kerensky in September. In this new
position, and despite his real sympathies,
Alexiev had been forced to order the arrest of
all conspirators implicated in Kornilov's coup.

Included amongst the prisoners with
Kornilov were Denikin and Generals
A. Lukomsky, I. Romanovsky and Sergei
Markov. These generals contemplated
the ensuing Bolshevik Revolution and the
future of their country while incarcerated
at Bykhov Monastery near Mogilev. Then,
learning that Alexiev had arrived in Don
Cossack territory on 15 November in order
to raise a volunteer army to fight the
Germans and Bolsheviks, the generals
decided to take action. Escaping from
the monastery, aided by loyal troops, on
2 December they made their way to the
Don separately and in disguise.

Here, in December, they met Alexiev
and the ataman of the Don Cossacks,
General A. Kaledin, to see about joint
resistance. The Revolution, however,

General Lavr Kornilov, *beau sabreur* of the White
movement in the south. Although short in stature,
his presence and command authority were as total
as his determination and bravery in combat.
(Dr Laurent Liguine collection)

General Mikhail Alexiev, founder of the Volunteer Army. Self-sacrificing, wise, experienced, and respected by the Allies, Alexiev's handling of the government, diplomacy and finance went far to save the Volunteer Army in 1918. (Dr Laurent Liguine collection)

had reached Cossack lands and Kaledin was not able to field a loyal army.

South Russia was in chaos. Revolutionary bands sacked homes and businesses and opened the jails to free political comrades and criminals alike. Nobles, officers and bourgeoisie were shot, sometimes on sight. Tens of thousands of Russian soldiers demobilized from the Caucasian Front thronged the cities, railheads and countryside. Now without orders and loitering without jobs, they learned of a revolution that promised all to those who had nothing. Many, hungry and desperate, went in search of food or easy money.

While Kornilov busied himself forming the new Volunteer Army, Alexiev used his extensive contacts to seek alliances and secure financing. The 'Volunteers', as they came to be known, recruited in the adjacent towns and surrounding areas of Rostov-on-Don (hereafter called Rostov), Taganrog and the Don Cossack capital, Novocherkassk. Nearly 4,000 joined between December 1917 and February 1918. The majority were officers

and teenagers from the Cadet and Junker military schools. In addition, General A. Bogaevsky had brought in a unit of Don Cossacks, and a band of women, survivors of the revolutionary massacres, joined as fighters and nursing sisters.

Meanwhile in January the Red Army had entered the Don. Kaledin, who had only been able to field one loyal unit, the elite Chernetsov Partisans, shot himself through the heart on 11 February. Eleven days later, deprived of an ally and facing an increasingly hostile city, Kornilov ordered his army to leave Rostov and head for the steppe country of the Kuban.

What followed was one of the epic events of military history, a campaign known by historians as the First Kuban Campaign and by veterans as the 'Ice March'. Over the next weeks, the Volunteers weathered snow and sleet, forded icy streams and rivers, and trudged through the late spring mud, while sleeping in the rough, eating scant rations and receiving half the minimum wage allotted to Bolshevik workers. Their arms and ammunition were what they carried with them, or what they could capture from the enemy.

During these weeks the Volunteers fought merely to stay alive against the overwhelming numbers of Red Guards sent to destroy them. The Reds established defences in towns while their troop trains and armoured trains travelled the rails attempting to locate and pin down the Volunteers. The Red Army in the south was estimated at 100,000 to 150,000 in those months. However, poor training and organization and lax discipline reduced their combat effectiveness.

In skirmish after battle, the Whites broke through the Reds, fording a river through sleet and darkness to take a town one day, advancing silently with fixed bayonets over an open field to take a position or a town on another. In 50 days they fought 40 actions. The number of killed always exceeded the number of wounded; nevertheless, the wounded were so numerous that over 1,200 had to be transported in peasant carts on the march. To leave anyone behind meant death.

Régiment Korniloff - 1919

The Kornilov Shock Regiment participated in the First Kuban Campaign, the 'Ice March', and in every major campaign on the Southern Front until November 1920. In 1919 the Kornilov Shock Division came closer to Moscow than any other White unit, fighting savage battles at Orel in September–October. (Allied art card, Bullock collection)

During this retreat, the Volunteers learned that the Don Cossacks had risen against the Bolsheviks. Moreover, Colonel Drozdovsky and 2,000 elite troops, who had just completed a 1,600-kilometre march across the Ukraine, joined the Volunteers in June. A steady trickle of officers and cadets from the north continued to arrive in these weeks so that by the middle of the month the Volunteer Army could field 9,000 men, three armoured cars and 21 guns. With the Cossacks anchoring his northern front, Denikin determined to strike southward and conquer the territories of the Caucasus and Kuban.

Second Kuban Campaign

The Second Kuban Campaign commenced on 23 June. The Reds were known to have 100,000 men in their North Caucasian Army stretched out along the towns and railways from south of Rostov to Stavropol and including their best units, Zhloba's Steel Division and the Taman Army Group. Denikin planned to advance southwest towards Ekaterinodar, knocking out Red garrisons ensconced on the railway, then continue to Novorossisk, liberating the ports along the eastern shore of the Black Sea. The Volunteers would then turn inland to attack Armavir and Stavropol in the northern Caucasus.

The Reds routinely mutilated then executed any Volunteer, while in turn the Whites usually shot Red prisoners out of hand.

In early April the Volunteers reached Ekaterinodar, the capital of the Kuban Cossacks, where they hoped to find allies. Like the Don, however, the Kuban had run red with revolution and the Bolsheviks were in control of the city.

At this point, Ataman Filimanov and 2,500 Kuban Cossacks under Colonel Pokrovsky rode in and joined the Volunteer Army. Encouraged, Kornilov decided on a desperate gamble: 6,000 Whites would try to wrest a city from 18,000 Red defenders armed with superior artillery and machine guns.

Over three days, from 10 to 13 April, the armies closed, often fighting hand-to-hand in the streets. The Volunteers lost over half their men. The Reds had suffered far more losses but were being reinforced daily. Finally, on the last day, an artillery shell struck headquarters, killing Kornilov. General Denikin, succeeding as commander-in-chief, decided to retreat north to reorganize and refit the army.

The first half of the plan went smoothly, concentric attacks by infantry and cavalry surrounding each rail station, with Shablievka, Torgovaya and Belaya Glina falling in turn. However, a shell fired from an armoured train killed General Markov, the gallant commander of the 1st Officers' Regiment, on 25 June. At Belaya Glina, the Whites began lining up Red prisoners, shooting the leaders and enlisting all others who agreed to volunteer. Hatred had

General Sergei Markov captures a Red troop train during the Second Kuban Campaign in 1918. Markov earned the sobriquet "General Forward" among his troops due to his daring and was always among the first to crack a joke in the field. (*Chasevoi émigré* journal, 1930)

intensified as more White prisoners were found horribly mutilated.

Next, 30,000 Red Guards were routed at Tikhoretskaya on 15 July, the Volunteers taking three armoured trains and 50 pieces of artillery; more importantly, the capture of this strategic rail hub severed Bolshevik communications with the north. Then, after a ten-day battle with the Taman Army

Group at Kushchevka, the Volunteers entered Ekaterinodar on 15 August.

The port of Novorossisk followed 11 days later, allowing volunteers from the Crimea to cross by ship to the liberated Kuban, volunteers such as the famed cavalry officer, General Baron Petr Nikolayevich Wrangel. Shortly after, Wrangel would command the 1st Cavalry Division. Another officer, General A. G. Shkuro, commander of the 'White Wolves' Kuban cavalry, had arrived at the end of July. By September, the army totalled 60,000.

Unfortunately, the architect of the Volunteer Army, General Alexiev, after

General Kutepov wearing the uniform of the elite
1st Officers' Regiment. Many of the men wore the red,
blue and white Volunteer Army chevron, point extended
downward, on the left sleeve from 1918 to early 1920.
A former Guards officer, Kutepov remained from the first
day of civil war to the last a highly competent, steady, and
thoroughly reliable commander always able to extract
the maximum military advantage from any situation.
(Dr Laurent Liguine collection)

Lieutenant-General V. L. Pokrovsky, former pilot in
World War One and holder of the St George Cross,
was a daring, resourceful commander of the Kuban
Cossacks. He was instrumental in the capture of
Tsaritsyn and Kamyshin in summer, 1919. However,
he was occasionally known as 'Hangman Pokrovsky' for
his strict discipline and tendency to hang Red prisoners.
(Deryabin collection)

suffering from cancer and pneumonia, died
on 8 October. His last words exhorted the
army to save Russia. Thereafter, Denikin
additionally assumed Alexiev's duties as
head of government, diplomacy and
finance, relegating these tasks on a
day-to-day basis to an advisory body
known as the Special Council.

The last half of the Second Kuban
Campaign consisted of intense battles at
Armavir and Stavropol, where the best and
most determined of the Reds had relocated.
The engagement at Armavir lasted ten days
in the middle of October while the action
at Stavropol lasted the first half of
November. General Drozdovsky was
mortally wounded at Stavropol at the
height of the action while leading his

2nd Officers' Regiment, while Wrangel's
cavalry forced the town, sabres drawn,
in a final *coup de main* on 15 November.

During the course of the year the Whites
had lost 30,000 men in battle.

Wrangel's 1st Cavalry Division had lost
260 officers and 2,460 men, or 100 per cent
of its original effective strength. Prince
Peter Volkonsky, writing from the
standpoint of 1919, perhaps stated it best.
At the battle of Armavir alone, the
1st Officers' General Markov Regiment
(renamed after its hero) suffered 50 per
cent casualties and the Composite Guards
Regiment 80 per cent. The greatest
casualties of all had occurred in the
Kornilov Shock Regiment, which could
only muster 500 men in late autumn,

The Don Cossacks struggled against the Red Army throughout 1918, from May under the leadership of General Krasnov. (Skobelev Committee art card, 1916, Bullock collection)

even though fully 5,000 had passed through its ranks in 1918.

Nevertheless, the Volunteers had survived, as had their Cossack hosts. The Armistice ending World War One seemed to hold much promise. Diplomatic contacts with the French and British seemed to indicate that troops and material assistance could be forthcoming. To Denikin, who had remained faithful to the Allies, this was a natural conclusion. As they looked forward to the Christmas of 1918, the Whites began speaking of Christmas 1919 in Moscow.

The Don Cossacks

The Red Army occupied the Don after the death of Ataman Kaledin in February. Entering Novocherskassk on 26 February, they shot his newly-elected successor, Ataman Nazarov. In response, General Popov

and 1,500 Cossacks escaped into the steppes to begin resistance. Meanwhile, the Bolshevik administration desecrated churches, burned farms and overturned the Cossack way of life; consequently, the Don rose in counter-revolution in April. On 16 May the Don council, or Krug, elected General Petr Krasnov as ataman. By June the Don flag of scarlet-yellow-blue had been hoisted and 40,000 Cossacks were under arms.

Krasnov now had to establish diplomatic ties with one or more of the competing powers surrounding his territory. The Reds were to his north and east and were hostile. The Volunteer Army to the south was friendly, but involved in campaigns in the Kuban. To the west, German troops were moving east, entering Don *voisko* (host territory) in April and May. By May the Germans had secured Taganrog, Rostov and the Donbas industrial region, areas which the Don Cossacks considered historically theirs or which they intended to expand into.

The Central Powers needed grain and coal and the Cossacks needed arms and artillery. Therefore, Krasnov struck a deal whereby both sides would receive what they needed and become, in essence, allied. This deal provoked the ire of Denikin who insisted on a pro-Allied stance. Nevertheless, Krasnov had made the only pragmatic decision open to him. During those months before the Armistice, the Allies were not in a position to support either Denikin or Krasnov.

By mid-August most of the *voisko* had been freed. The army had stood briefly at 50,000, nearly three-quarters consisting of cavalry. Aircraft, armoured car and armoured train units were under formation. In August, the Cossacks made their first abortive bid to take Tsaritsyn on the Volga. Tsaritsyn was important as the gateway to the Caucasus and Central Asia, as the conduit through which Red forces were supplied and through which vital food passed on their way to hungry Bolshevik-controlled cities in the north.

In September, the Cossacks tried again and succeeded in nearly surrounding the city before being pushed back to the Don. The third attack, commencing on 3 December,

lasted into January 1919. The Cossacks came under mounting pressure from the Red 8th and 9th Armies on their northern front and a heavily reinforced 10th Army at Tsaritsyn.

Cavalry and armoured car of the Central Rada attack Bolshevik positions in Kiev during the Arsenal uprising, February 1918. The Ukrainian cavalry is wearing light blue and yellow armbands. (Bullock photo, sectional from painting, Arsenal Museum, Kiev)

The Ukraine

The February Revolution of 1917 had unleashed Ukrainian aspirations for a nationalist state free of Russian control, while the Bolshevik October Revolution provided an immediate context for a complete break. On 20 November, the representative council known as the Central Rada, headed by Mykhailo Hrushevsky, declared independence and the formation of the Ukrainian National Republic, an entity socialist in nature but non-Bolshevik.

After eliminating forces loyal to the Russian Provisional Government, the Rada next faced a Bolshevik rebellion at the Kiev arsenal and a subsequent invasion by Red Guards based at Kharkov. At this time, just prior to the Treaty of Brest-Litovsk, the Central Powers were continuing to advance across the Ukraine. Seeking assistance against the Reds, the Rada

concluded an alliance with the Germans on 9 February. Nevertheless, after the Germans established control at Kiev and key centres in the Ukraine, they overturned the Rada on 29 April, installing a more malleable regime under Pavel Skoropadsky.

Skoropadsky adopted the title 'Hetman', or 'leader', his government becoming known as the 'Ukrainian State', or more popularly as the 'Hetmanate'. Despite the many colourfully uniformed Ukrainian units raised, from the start the Hetmanate was dependent on German arms and military assistance.

In exchange, Skoropadsky had to deliver large quantities of food. This led the Hetman to favour the landowners who could supply shipments of victuals for the German war machine over the interests of the peasantry, thereby making him unpopular in the countryside. This policy, in fact, led to large-scale agrarian unrest. Additionally,

Hetman Pavel Skoropadsky, 29 May 1918. (Photo card issued 1918, Kiev, Bullock collection)

Skoropadsky antagonized Ukrainian nationalists because he favoured an eventual union with a non-Bolshevik Russia.

Skoropadsky's fortunes waned when the Central Powers began withdrawing after the Armistice of November 1918. An uprising led by Simon Petlyura overthrew the Hetmanate that November, re-establishing, at least in name, the Urkrainian National Republic. Real power, however, resided in a five-man body known as the Directory, a body dedicated to moderate socialism and Ukrainian independence.

Eastern Front

On 14 May 1918 a Russian train loaded with Austro-Hungarian prisoners of war pulled alongside a troop train of the Czech Legion in Chelyabinsk. Insults were traded and a Hungarian hurled a piece of metal across the tracks, wounding a Czech. In response, a unit of legionnaires mobbed the train and lynched the Hungarian. In a matter of weeks, this fit of pique, the 'Chelyabinsk Incident', changed the world.

Troops of what would become known as the Czech Legion (or more properly the Czechoslovak Legion) had been serving in the imperial Russian Army since the

Czech soldiers atop an armoured train. (© Corbis)

outbreak of World War One in 1914. Most were deserters from the Austro-Hungarian Army, which was at war with Russia. During the course of the war the Allied powers had promised the Czechs a new homeland in Europe, Czechoslovakia, to be carved out of the Austro-Hungarian domain. Understandably, the Austro-Hungarians considered those in the Legion to be traitors, hanging them when caught.

The Czech Legion in Samara, capital of the KOMUCH government, in June 1918. The author stayed in Samara in 1999 and found the waterfront and old city remarkably unchanged. (Photo card, Bullock collection)

Since the fall of the Russian Provisional Government in 1917, the Legion had been trying to get out of Russia in order to reinforce the French on the Western Front and thereby make a contribution to the Allied war effort. At first, the Bolsheviks facilitated the evacuation so that they could get this 50,000-strong, armed body out of the way and get on with consolidating their revolution. Then, bowing to German pressure that the Czechs should be disarmed and not be allowed to reach the West, they began to impede that evacuation. Exacerbating the situation were the hundreds of thousands of German, Austro-Hungarian and Turkish prisoners of war still inside Russia whom the Czechs considered enemies. From March to May tension increased as the Legion began to distrust the real intentions of the Bolsheviks and especially their connections with the Germans, real and imagined. Rather than completely disarm, the Legion revolted on 25 May.

In one of the most remarkable feats in military history, the Legion began overpowering one Bolshevik garrison after another: Chelyabinsk on the 26th, Penza on the 28th and Simbirsk on 30 May; Samara on the 8th and Ufa on 23 June. This consolidated their positions on the Volga River. Other units pressed east along

the Trans-Siberian Railway, taking Omsk and Irkutsk, and finally reaching Vladivostok and the Pacific Ocean by the end of August. Within three months, the Czechs had conquered more territory than any other power in World War One (for more detail on these adventures, see Osprey's Men-at-Arms 447, *The Czech Legion*).

The unseating of Bolshevik power on the Volga and across Siberia heralded the genesis of the White movement in the east. Although some 19 governments arose in these regions, the most important were the establishment of the Committee of Members of the Constituent Assembly (KOMUCH) on 1 June and the Provisional Government of Siberia (PSG) at Omsk on the 30th.

The KOMUCH government was Socialist Revolutionary (SR) in temperament and flew a red flag; however, the government was staunchly anti-Bolshevik. More than any other political entity, this government most represented the will of the people as expressed in the elections of 1917. Many had fled from Petrograd after Lenin dissolved the Constituent Assembly in January 1918.

Determined to capture and hold the Volga region, KOMUCH ordered a general mobilization of troops into what would be known as the 'People's Army'. A few volunteer formations of officers and partisans had already come forward at the beginning, including the 1st Samara Volunteer Detachment led by the heroic and talented Colonel (later General) Vladimir Oskarovich Kappel. However, only 30,000 local recruits responded to military conscription. Most of these arrived with no military training and half could not be supplied with arms.

Despite these handicaps, the next weeks were filled with optimism. Overall command of the KOMUCH forces fell on Colonel Galkin while Kappel built up a force of 2,000, styled the Special Independent Rifle Brigade, replete with component cavalry, mortars and artillery. Kappel took Syzran and Stavropol (modern Togliatti) in early July and Simbirsk on the 22nd. Colonel

Fall of KOMUCH

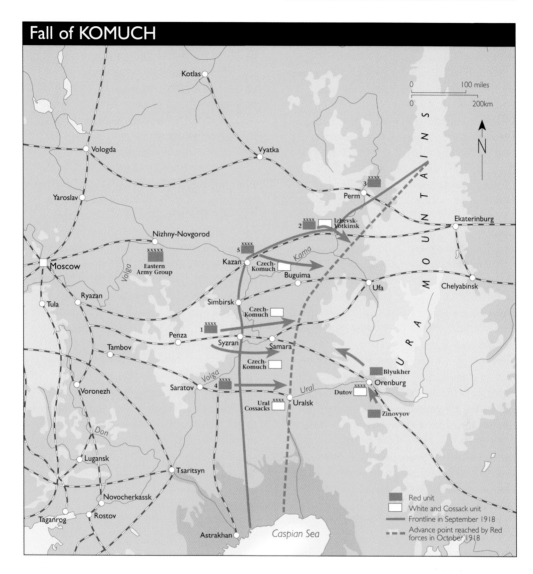

(later General) Voitsekhovsky followed this with the seizure of Ekaterinburg on 25 July. Voitsekhovksy, who would become another of the Whites' heroes in Siberia, unfortunately arrived too late to save the tsar and his family. Agents of the Cheka had slaughtered them in the basement of the Ipatiev House on the 16th to prevent their rescue.

Other forces toppled the weak Bolshevik administrations throughout the region. In the south, General A. I. Dutov, ataman of the Orenburg Cossacks, took Orenburg in July. In the north, Colonel V. M. Molchanov raised 7,500 volunteers in Viatka province.

Meanwhile, on 7 July, at the behest of KOMUCH and the Allies, the Czechs had agreed to consolidate the majority of their troops on the Volga to constitute an eastern front against the Central Powers and the Bolsheviks. General S. K. Cecek, commander of the Legion's 1st Division at Ufa, headed the newly constituted 'Volga Front'. The Legion co-located their own units with those of KOMUCH and drilled the Russian conscripts. That month, liaison officers signalled to the Legion that major landings of Allied troops at Archangel and Vladivostok were imminent.

Moving north towards the Allies, a joint expedition of the 1st Czechoslovak Regiment, Kappel's Russians and a KOMUCH aviation detachment proceeded up the Volga by steamer and captured Kazan on 6 August. The Russians disembarked and attacked on the west, the Legion coming in from the east. The Red Guards panicked and left behind the tsar's imperial gold reserve, a fabulous fortune in gold assets (two-thirds of a billion gold roubles, or approximately 25 billion current US dollars) that the Bolsheviks had moved to Kazan in May for 'safekeeping'.

Encouraged by the fall of nearby Kazan, thousands of middle-class workers at the factories of Izhevsk and Votkinsk in the Kama River Valley revolted against Bolshevik domination. In time, these workers would become one of the White Army's most hard-hitting military forces. These summer days of August, filled with celebrations and hope, were the halcyon days of KOMUCH.

KOMUCH's good fortune was largely due to the weakness of the Red Army on the western bank of the Volga and their surprise at the rapid collapse of their authority in Siberia. The People's Army needed more officers, but these were offered better pay and conditions of service by the Provisional Government of Siberia at Omsk. Politically, the PSG was right of centre and better suited the inclinations of the officer corps. This prejudice carried over into political affairs, causing the PSG to withhold its military forces from the People's Army. Although the Allies were pressing the two governments to combine in a united front, negotiations stalled.

By September, General Rudolf Gaida's Czechoslovak 2nd Division had reinforced the Volga Front, headquartered at Ekaterinburg. The total forces available to KOMUCH, counting all partisan units and groups on the northern and southern flanks, were 77,000. Against these, the Reds deployed the five armies of their Eastern Group: from north to south, the 3rd, the 2nd, the 5th, the 1st and the 4th, a total of 70,000 in mid-September, rising to 103,000 in early October, including the elite Latvian Division. Moreover, the Red Turkestan group of 12,000 and Vasily Blyukher's South Urals Partisan Army of 10,000 were engaging Dutov in the south near Orenburg, Blyukher's partisans linking up with the Reds on the Volga in September.

Red armoured train on the Ural Front, spring 1918. (Photo, Bullock collection)

End of a dynasty

The Romanov dynasty lasted from 1613 to 1917. Nicholas II (1868–1918) acceded to the throne of the Russian Empire in 1894. In many ways, Nicholas was like King Louis XVI of France, a devoted family man attuned more to private life than the epic events fate thrust upon him. Both were out of step with their contemporary world, both faced revolutions, and both in the end proved unequal to their historical tasks and suffered the ultimate consequence.

Nicholas' wife, the Tsarina Alexandra Fedorovna (her given Russian name), was the German Princess Alix of Hesse-Darmstadt (1872–1918) and granddaughter of Britain's Queen Victoria. Nicholas himself was cousin to both George V of Britain, to whom he bore an uncanny resemblance, and to Kaiser Wilhelm II of Germany. Nicholas and Alexandra had four daughters, Olga, Tatiana, Maria and Anastasia, and one son, Alexei.

The royal family fell into public disrepute through their association with the dissolute and scandalous 'holy man', Grigory Yekfimovich Novikh, more popularly known as 'Rasputin'. Rasputin received royal favour because of his ability to heal the young Tsarevich Alexei, who was a supposed victim of haemophilia or uncontrolled bleeding. At the time, the exact nature of the disease was kept so secret that the actual diagnosis has remained controversial to the present day.

Military reverses at the front in World War One also shook public confidence in the Romanov dynasty, as did food shortages that emerged in the winter of 1916/17. Under mounting revolutionary pressure and with the encouragement of his primary advisors, Nicholas abdicated the throne on 15 March 1917.

Initially under house arrest at their residence, the Alexander Palace at Tsarkoe Selo, the Royal Family was moved to the Kornilov House in Tobolsk, Siberia, in August 1917. They were moved again to the Ipatiev House in Ekaterinburg in the Urals in two groups in April and May 1918. A special squad of Cheka agents under Yakov Yurovsky arrived to superintend the Royal Family in early July.

Although none of the White Armies declared for the Tsar's reinstatement, the rescue of the Royal Family, for the sake of honor and decency, was their concern as well as the concern of the Allied governments, and even Imperial Germany. As White troops and the Czech Legion converged on Ekaterinburg to rescue the prisoners, the Bolsheviks took hard and decisive action. Eschewing the international show trial they had desired in Moscow, the Moscow Soviet (including the key Bolshevik leadership) ordered the local Ural Soviet to dispose of the Royal prisoners. The royal family, together with the family companions Dr. Eugene Botkin and Anna Demidova, as well as the loyal male retainers Trupp and Kharitinov, were all killed. Olga was 22, Tatiana 21, Maria 19, Anastasia 17, and the Tsarevich Alexei 13.

The Royal Family: (top row, left to right) Grand Duchess Olga, Tsarina Aleksandra, (bottom row, left to right) Grand Duchess Maria, Tsar Nicholas II, Grand Duchess Anastasia, Tsarevich Alexei, Grand Duchess Tatiana. (Bullock Collection)

Admiral Alexander Vasilievich Kolchak, 'Supreme Ruler of All the Russias', November 1918 through to February 1920. (Tobie Mathew collection)

Suitably reinforced, the Reds opened a general offensive on 8 September along a 500-kilometre front from Kazan to Simbirsk. After desultory fighting in Kazan, KOMUCH forces evacuated the city by steamer or overland by cart on the 9th, the city falling the next day. Simbirsk followed on the 12th. The front began to crumble as the conscripts of summer began to desert.

Under pressure politically as well as militarily, KOMUCH agreed to unite with the PSG at the Ufa Conference on 23 September. The new political entity, the 'All Russian Provisional Government', more popularly known as 'The Directory', would be seated at Omsk in western Siberia. This agreement effectively subordinated KOMUCH under the PSG. The question became academic when Samara, the capital of KOMUCH, fell to the Reds on 8 October.

The next five weeks of the Directory were spent saving the front. The PSG, flying the white-over-green flag of Siberia (white snow over the green *taiga*), had mustered 30,000–40,000 troops of its own in the months prior to union. The addition of these troops essentially replaced the losses and desertions suffered by the People's Army. General V. G. Boldyrev, a political moderate and a member of the five-man Directory leadership, commanded the front.

Two actions saved the Whites along the foothills of the Ural Mountains that autumn. In the centre of the line, Voitsekhovsky declared martial law in Ufa on 15 October. Rallying Legion troops, he advanced west against the main Red spearhead moving east from Simbirsk and Samara. Kappel, moving east from the Simbirsk sector, struck the Reds from behind at Belebei. This halted their offensive and freed 15,000 survivors of the People's Army trapped behind enemy lines. In the north, Molchanov's Brigade and the Izhevsk-Votkinsk rebels, a group of 15,000, fought their way through the Red lines just below Perm.

Politically, however, the Directory was in trouble. Right-of-centre elements, disturbed by conditions at the front, decried any socialist influence in the government, however moderate. Political manoeuvring, hardening positions and rumours of an impending coup had cursed the Directory from the beginning. On the night of 17/18 November, key Russian officers in Omsk arrested the members of the Directory and installed Admiral Alexander Vasilievich Kolchak as 'Supreme Ruler of All the Russias'.

The details behind this event have remained controversial to the present. According to Boldyrev, General Maurice Janin (head of the French Military Mission) and subsequent Soviet history, Kolchak and the British Military Mission in Omsk engineered the coup. The truth is more subtle. The British had been apprised of proceedings by Russian agents. On the night of the coup, they protected the admiral with teams of machine gunners. Kolchak, when asked if would accept the mantle of 'dictatorship' if the offer arose, had gravely consented for patriotic reasons, in order to save Russia.

The devil hid in the details of unfolding events – who, when, where, how much. In the end, a local plurality of Russian officers and politicians, after becoming disenchanted with the inefficiency and military ineptitude of successive 'socialist' regimes – from Kerensky to KOMUCH to the Directory – took direct action themselves.

The man they chose to elevate as Supreme Ruler was widely respected in Russian and Allied circles. Kolchak had been born in St Petersburg in 1873, the son of a naval engineer. After graduating from the Naval Academy in 1894 he won acclaim from the scientific community for his work in oceanography and hydrology. He followed this up in 1900 with a three-year exploration of the Arctic. Immediately after, he participated in the Russo-Japanese War, directing the laying of minefields at Port Arthur.

Kolchak served in World War One, attaining the rank of rear admiral and command of the Black Sea Fleet in July 1916. He won national attention after the February Revolution in 1917 when he defiantly threw his sword overboard rather than submit to the demands of the sailors' councils. The Americans then asked Kolchak to tour naval facilities in the United States and Kerensky approved the tour in July. After meeting President Wilson, Kolchak sailed for home through the Pacific, stopping in Japan. There, he learned of the Bolshevik Revolution and promptly offered his services to the British ambassador in Tokyo.

Before the British could effectively utilize him, however, the Russian ambassador in Peking requested he join General

Red cavalry enters Kazan, October 1918. (Photo, Deryabin collection, c. 1920s)

D. L. Horvathat Harbin, China. Horvath was assembling an army of anti-Bolsheviks in northern Manchuria to fight in the Russian Far East. From April 1918 until September, Kolchak tried and failed to form a credible coalition between White elements in the Far East or to establish cooperative relations with Japan.

Frustrated, he left Vladivostok on 21 September and headed for the front in the west. Almost immediately after arriving in Omsk on 13 October, the Directory placed him in charge of the Ministries of the Army and the Navy. On 9 November he began a tour of the front in his new capacity, returning on the evening of the 16th, scarcely a day before the coup.

On 18 November he made his first speech as Supreme Ruler, which made a profound impression on the Russians as well as the Allies from whom he sought diplomatic recognition. As quoted in the work of Serge Petroff: 'I will not go down the path of reaction, nor the ruinous path of party politics ... my main goal is to create a battle-worthy army, attain a victory over Bolshevism, and establish law and order so that the people may without prejudice choose for themselves the manner of government which they prefer.'

Red baptism of fire

In the first months, the Bolsheviks were able to put down counter-revolutionary uprisings easily enough. Most challenges were only from half-hatched political plots, armed gangs or groups of the discontented. Three challenges were potentially more serious, those of Dutov, Kaledin and Kornilov. Armoured trains and troop trains overloaded with Red Guards overturned Ataman Dutov's Orenburg Cossacks in January 1918, taking his capital on the 31st of that month. Red Guards converging south from Kharkhov and north from the Causcasus similarly defeated Ataman Kaledin's Don Cossacks in February. Kornilov's Volunteer Army was too small to be considered a serious threat.

A. Z. Zhelezniakov, an Anarchist sailor who fought the Don Cossacks in 1918. In 1919 he commanded a formation of armoured trains against Denikin. (Painting by L. Kotliarov, Sovietsky Kudoshnik art card, 1960s)

The revolt of the Czech Legion in May jolted any feelings of complacency. The collapse of Bolshevik administrations throughout Siberia was a shock further compounded by the loss of influence along the Volga when KOMUCH began armed opposition in June. The loss of Kazan on 6 August was the final challenge that set Commissar for War Trotsky in motion. Kappel's Whites and the Czechs had captured the immense Romanov Bridge that spanned the Volga and had interposed themselves between the Red 1st and 2nd Armies. From this point, the Whites could advance on Moscow or possibly link with the Allies who had begun landings in the north at Archangel.

Setting out from Moscow in his armoured train with a full staff retinue, Trotsky arrived at Sviazhsk station, 60 kilometres from Kazan. This railway station barred the way to Moscow. It was here, over the next month, that Trotsky formed the first of his reliable and more regular armies, the 5th Army.

Punishment for the loss of Kazan and the imperial gold was immediate. Trotsky ordered the shooting of the commander and commissar, and lined up and decimated, in full Roman fashion, units that had panicked. Similar discipline was applied to the personnel of the monitors, river barges and armoured steamers of the Volga Flotilla, under Commander Raskolnikov, including its flagship the *Ilya Mouromets*. Four naval destroyers were brought in as reinforcements. Reserves were transferred from the west and rallied around his one reliable unit, the 5th Latvian Semigallian Soviet Regiment.

Meanwhile, advance elements of the 2nd Army moved northeast against the Kazan defenders on 24 August in support of the 5th Army. Aircraft, armoured cars and ships of both sides skirmished over the next days, but the Whites and Czechs, being greatly outnumbered, evacuated the city on 9 September. Three days later, to the south, Simbirsk fell to Mikhail Tukachevsky's First Army. There an armoured train and Comrade Gai's 'Iron Division' forced the bridge across the Volga. By October, the Eastern Front had been restored and the enemy government, KOMUCH, destroyed. According to Soviet legend, the Red Army had found its feet during the weeks at Kazan.

The stand at Tsaritsyn (later Stalingrad, now Volgograd) became an even more famous legend once Stalin was able to reshape history in the 1930s. This city on the Volga, 875 kilometres from Moscow, was the strategic linchpin of the Red line in the southeast. As long as the Reds held Tsaritsyn, the Whites in the east could not link up with the Whites of the south and southwest. Conversely, the city anchored the Red right flank on the Eastern Front and provided supplies and reinforcements to Red armies operating in the northern Caucasus and at Astrakhan, a city situated farther south on the Volga abutting the Caspian Sea.

Economically, the railways converging on Tsaritsyn transmitted cotton, food and other commodities from Central Asia to the Bolshevik heartland in the centre. If Kazan won Trotsky's election to Soviet sainthood, Tsaritsyn achieved Stalin's.

Commissar Stalin arrived in Tsaritsyn with two armoured cars and 400 bodyguards on 6 June. By September, he had become Special Commissar to the entire Southern Army Group, consisting of the 8th, 9th, 10th and 11th Armies. From the start, Stalin shook up the command structures, arguing with Trotsky over the role of the military specialists and appointing his own men at will. Two men he chose to back, who would become his lifelong supporters, were Kliment Voroshilov and Semyon Budenny.

That spring, Voroshilov had organized the Lugansk Red Guard and had carried out a spectacular fighting retreat to Tsaritsyn, hounded by the Germans and Don Cossacks. Handsome, cunning, an excellent horseman

Red commander Kliment Efremovich Voroshilov in the trenchworks at Tsaritsyn, 1918. (Painting by L. Kotliarov, Soviet art card, c. 1930)

Admiral Kolchak's capital at Omsk on the Irtysh River.
(Bullock collection)

and crack pistol shot, Voroshilov was
popular with the younger troops and
would hold several important posts as army
commander and commissar throughout the
civil war. Semyon Budenny, a former tsarist
cavalry non-commissioned officer and
recipient of all St George awards for bravery,
would rise to command the 1st Horse Army
or *Konarmiya* in 1919. Together with Stalin,
these men and other like-minded associates
would form the 'Tsaritsyn Clique', a group
that would profoundly affect Soviet history.

Stalin received credit for successfully
defending Tsaritsyn from three Don
Cossack offensives that took place in August,
September and finally from December 1918
to January 1919. Far from facing
overwhelming odds as their reports indicated,
the Reds had a marked superiority in artillery,
machine guns and armoured trains and their
forces rose from a rough numerical parity
with the Cossacks to a distinct superiority by
January. However, he did not manage to save
the North Caucasian Army that Denikin's
Volunteers progressively destroyed that
autumn, nor to avert the catastrophe
that would befall in spring 1919.

1919

Kolchak's offensive

In the weeks after Kolchak's ascension, the front stabilized along the Urals and morale improved dramatically. The Izhevsk and Votkinsk Brigades, Molchanov's Brigade and Kappel's troops formed the nucleus of the new Western Army in the centre. The imperial gold had successfully arrived in Chelyabinsk from Samara in November, soon to be transferred to Omsk. The Whites desired an early offensive, even in winter, to throw the Reds off balance, understanding that they were growing in strength. Early success could also bring diplomatic recognition from the Allies, and, just as importantly, much-needed supplies.

In December 1918, General Gaida, having resigned from the Legion and accepted command of the Siberian Army in Russian service, moved against the Red 3rd Army at Perm. The city fell on the 25th, yielding a rich haul of 20,000 prisoners, 20 staff cars, 5,000 train wagons and stock, 60 guns, 1,000 machine guns and several armoured trains. Local intelligence reports described the 3rd Army as 'annihilated'. Partially offsetting this, the Reds pushed back the Whites in the south, taking Ufa on 31 December and Uralsk and Orenburg in January 1919.

Kolchak now ordered a general mobilization throughout Siberia, with about 200,000 responding to the call. Many of these recruits were located in garrisons along the lines of communications that stretched for 8,000 kilometres from the front to the Pacific. Others entered into various training establishments. According to arrangements among the Allies, the British had control of the 'rear', which meant overseeing and advising the Whites about the administration of supplies and the training of new recruits.

The British advised Kolchak to call up only the number of men who could be armed, suitably attired, fed and lodged in decent quarters, then trained for a minimum of two months. In order to build cadres for the Whites, the British established a Training Brigade on Russian Island, off the Pacific port of Vladivostok, where such a regime could be carried out. Each 'class' could graduate 3,000 soldiers at a time, including officers and non-commissioned officers. Each platoon had a Russian officer, the commander of each company also being Russian, but with a British supervisor. The command, at battalion level and up, would be in British hands. After two months, a fresh crop of 3,000 would rotate in, fully equipped.

The purpose was to create a bond between the young officers and the new conscripts by having them train together. The British described the potential of the average

Kolchak troops in British caps, coats and equipment, but with Russian boots and cockades, spring 1919. (Bullock collection)

Kolchak's offensive

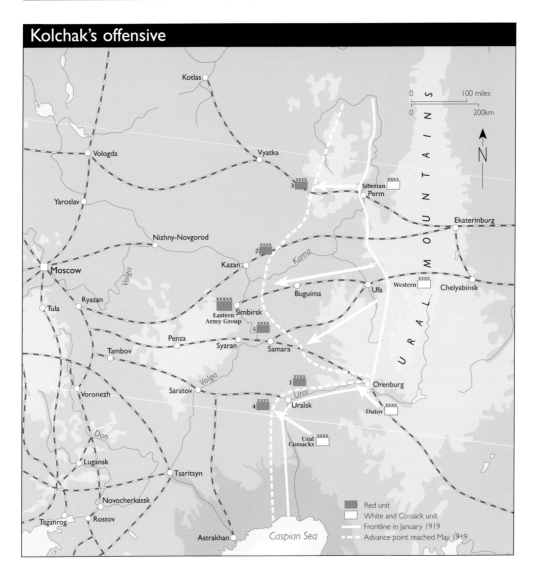

Siberian recruits as 'excellent', but noted that
their performance and morale were quickly
degraded by company-level officers who had
not established a critical rapport with their
men. Lacking supplies and care, or a clear
understanding of why they were expected to
fight, the troops naturally preferred to return
to their homes. For example, the Russians
packed one new regiment onto trains,
bounced it around on the tracks for
six weeks without necessary food and
equipment, then halted near the front.
Upon disembarking, the entire unit deserted.

The Whites, on the other hand, felt the
urgent need to send all troops to the front

quickly, either as fresh drafts to replace
casualties or to plug gaps in the line.
Two British training experiments just behind
the front, the Anglo-Russian Brigade and
Kappel's Corps, failed for these very reasons.
The Anglo-Russian Brigade, which received
Kolchak's approval, was the first of several
planned units with mixed Russian and British
officers and instructors, the British taking
a particularly prominent role in forming
machine-gun companies and batteries
of artillery. The first battalion showed great
promise but became the jealous object of scorn
from senior Russian officers who broke up the
establishment at the earliest opportunity.

The other scheme involved processing the mass levies raised during the general mobilization. Eight divisions were to be created, three as components of Kappel's Corps, the other five based at regional centres. These were to be fully equipped and trained before being sent into battle. Owing to urgency at the front, however, the regional centres were pared down to three, and even these were disbanded prematurely to get troops into the forward sectors. The White command, or *stavka*, then committed Kappel's divisions to combat before they were ready.

As more White units reached the Ural Front, the Czech Legion withdrew its troops along the lines of communications, setting up small garrisons from Ekaterinburg and Chelyabinsk to such faraway locations as Barnaul and Harbin. The entire Trans-Siberian Railway and the spur lines to the north and south were effectively under Legion control. These garrisons were supported by, or worked in coordination with, the various other Allied powers who had similar garrisons at strategic locations.

Czech Legion patrol in the Urals, early 1919. (Legion painting, 1926)

Kolchak ordered his spring offensive to begin in March, despite the snow in the Ural passes. His main objective was to attain and consolidate the Volga. Thereafter, the armies would move directly on Moscow from the centre, or adopt a north–centre strategy if linking with the Allies in North Russia proved feasible, or even a centre–south strategy if conditions looked auspicious for linking with Denkin's Armed Forces of South Russia.

In theory, each White army would comprise 50,000 infantry and cavalry in two corps, with two or three divisions and a reserve brigade in each. In reality, the armies were much under-strength, and stretched along a 1,100-kilometre line from Perm to Orenburg. On the left, the front extended still further to the Caspian Sea.

On the right, or farthest north of the line, stood Gaida's Siberian Army with headquarters at Ekaterinburg. The largest of the armies, Gaida's had 45,000 men, the majority being the new recruits. His troops would advance against the Red 3rd and 2nd Armies with the objective of taking Viatka.

General M. V. Khanzin's Western Army anchored the centre with headquarters at Chelyabinsk. Khanzin, possessing 42,000 men, would advance against the Red 1st and 5th Armies to capture Samara and Ufa and consolidate the central Volga region. Kappel's Corps, still under formation, would reinforce the Western Army as the offensive unfolded.

General Belov's Southern Army, situated on the left of the line, was the smallest, with perhaps 20,000–30,000 men. Belov would protect Khanzin's left flank by grappling with the Red 1st Army, while offering support to the Orenburg Cossacks on his own left flank.

Two Cossack armies worked to the south of Belov. Ataman Dutov's Orenburg Cossacks, headquartered near Orenburg, had an approximate strength of 15,000. Dutov would advance from Orsk and take Orenburg while severing the Tashkent Railway, thereby cutting off the Red Turkestan Army from the main Red forces to the northwest. Ataman Tolstoy's 15,000 Ural Cossacks, with their left flank on the Caspian Sea, would direct their attention on the Red 4th Army and capturing Uralsk.

Overall, the Whites had a nearly five-to-four numerical advantage over their enemy's 118,000. However, the Reds had greater artillery and machine gun assets and much larger reserves in their immediate interior, and a field army in Turkestan operating to the southeast of the White lines.

The general offensive opened across the entire front between 4 and 13 March, taking the enemy by surprise. Khanzin's army moved on horse-drawn sledges over snows over half a metre in depth, breaking through the Red 5th Army and securing Ufa on the 16th. His cavalry pursued the Reds to Belebei. Sterlitamak followed on 6 April, allowing Dutov to recapture Orsk on the 9th and proceed to within 32 kilometres of Orenburg. Gaida's Siberian Army pressed forward on skis to Glazov, taking Sarapul on

the Kama River on the 11th. By the middle of April the Western Army had captured Bugulma and Buguruslan, opening the way to Samara and Simbirsk.

The end of April became the high-water mark of the White advance, Khanzin having gained 550 kilometres in the centre. For two weeks the Whites had been stuck in seas of mud that developed in the spring thaw, giving the enemy time to recover. Moreover, the Siberian Army had moved too far to the northwest while the Western Army had advanced too far to the southwest, creating a dangerous gap in between. As Gaida neared Kazan in early May, the sodden ground started to harden and the Red Army counter-attacked.

The Reds directed their main effort against Khanzin's centre and on his northern and southern flanks, exploiting the gaps that had developed as well as taking advantage of command-and-control weaknesses that naturally develop between armies on the move. Hard-pressed, the Western Army fell back on Ufa and the Belaia River line. On 7 June the Red 5th Army, spearheaded by Vasily Chapaev's legendary 25th Division, loaded onto barges and crossed below Ufa, creating a bridgehead. The Whites committed their shock brigade in a desperate, bloody attempt to prevent the line from crumpling. Nevertheless, by mid-June the Western Army had been pushed back 80 kilometres.

In the north, the Red 2nd and 3rd Armies, cooperating with the heavily armed Volga Flotilla, captured Perm on 1 July. Gaida's Siberians fell back in disarray to and then beyond Ekaterinburg by 15 July. Desertions among his new recruits were particularly high. In the south, the Orenburg and Ural Cossacks made only limited headway. The hosts were still disorganized after the loss of Orenburg and Uralsk in January and the defection of the Allied 'Bashkir Corps' in February.

In response, Kolchak shook up his command, placing the steady General M. K. Dieterichs in charge of the front on 20 June. On 8 July, he removed Gaida, and the Siberian Army became the 1st Army under General Anatoly Pepelyaev. Khanzin was also

The Russian Civil War and cinematography

Stills from the 1934 Lenfilm movie production *Chapaev* (*100 Soviet Films*. Iskusstvo: Moscow, 1967). In this scene, Kolchak's White Guards advance silently with fixed bayonets into withering machine-gun fire and are annihilated. The uniforms of black and white have a large black patch on the left arm, bordered white (with a white Orthodox-style cross, and just above, an inscription in white, both in the patch centre). Their black flag bears a white skull and crossbones with the inscription 'God with Us' superimposed. In the film, Red soldiers verbally warn their comrades of the attack of this 'Kappelevtsi Officer's Regiment'. This scene recreates an actual battle on 8 June 1919 when an officers' shock regiment, each man previously having won the St George Cross for bravery, attempted to save the city of Ufa. In his memoirs, the adjutant of Red Commander Frunze recalled the 'terrifying impression' made by General Kappel's shock battalions advancing on their positions 'with the skull and crossbones insignia mounted on their caps, sleeves, and epaulettes' (Bubnov et al., *Grazhdanskaia Voina*, vol. 3, 1928). Another eyewitness, Dmitry Furmanov, Red commissar to Chapaev's famed 25th Division, had received intelligence the evening before that 'two battalions of officers and the Kappel Regiment' were to attack at dawn. He recalled:

> *In black columns, in ghostly silence, without sound of human voice or clatter of arms, the battalions of officers and the Kappel Regiment advanced to the attack. They came on in open order, covering an enormous space ... the battalions were allowed to come up quite close, and then, at the word of command, scores of machine-guns blazed fire. Their work was gruesome. They mowed down the Whites in swathes, line after line, wiped them out.*
> (*Chapaev*, Martin Lawrence Ltd, London, 1935, pp. 278–79).

At the end of that day of slaughter, nearly 3,000 of Kolchak's finest lay dead.

Days before the battle, foreign observers, including the Dutch correspondent Ludovic Grondijs, had reported elite shock units, bedecked with 'death's head insignia', marching through the streets of Chelyabinsk *en route* to the front. Based on White orders of battle, these units belonged to the Shock Brigade of General Kappel's Volga Corps, the brigade that attacked at Ufa.

An historical question remains, when tying the film and book to the actual events. Were the incredibly detailed uniforms only a Soviet epitome of what a White Guard unit *should* look like, or were they based in whole or part on captured uniforms? The answer may lie in the archives of Lenfilm, the former Soviet studio owned since 2004 by Filmofond PJSC.

To the Urals

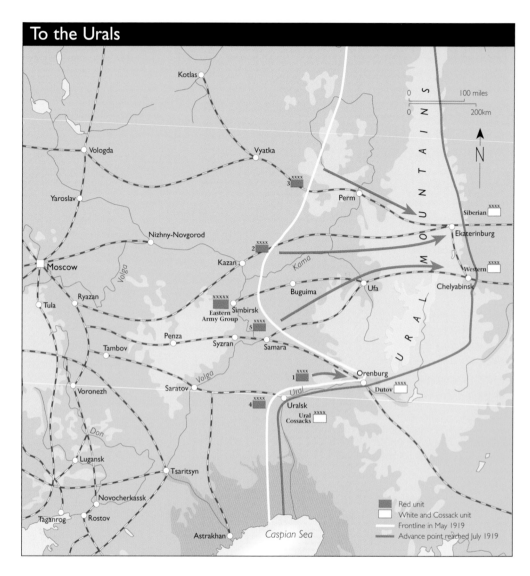

removed, the Western Army reorganizing into two: the 2nd Army under General A. N. Lokhvitsky and the 3rd Army under General K. V. Sakharov.

As the Whites retired, the armies began melting away, the conscripts deserting to their villages. Zlatoust fell on 13 July, bringing the Red 5th Army over the Urals to Chelyabinsk. Here the Whites planned an elaborate manoeuvre. The 5th Army would be allowed into the city and then encircled. For eight days, from 23 to 31 July, the battle raged.

Chelyabinsk held because the factory workers of the city revolted and joined the defences while the Red 3rd Army moved

southeast from Ekaterinburg against the Whites' right flank. Even though the Whites inflicted 11,000 casualties on the Reds while only losing 5,000 themselves, thousands of conscripts deserted from Kappel's Volga Corps, proving the general unreliability of the troops mobilized that spring. In the end, the Whites continued to fall back, giving up the entire Ural line.

The Whites retreated across the immense western Siberian plain in August to the Tobol River, hoping to rally and make a stand. But the Reds retained the initiative. Finally, 350 kilometres from the Tobol, the Whites reached the Ishim River, itself only 225 kilometres from their capital at Omsk. Here, the Red offensive blew itself out.

True to the fluidity of operations in the Russian Civil War, offensive and counter-offensive, after two weeks the Whites were in position to strike back. Kolchak determined to counter-attack in order to support the offensives of the Whites in south and northwest Russia that were already under way or about to begin. The immediate objective was the Tobol River line, the grander goal being the recovery of the Urals.

On 1 September, the 1st and 2nd Armies moved against the Red 3rd Army while the White 3rd attacked the Red 5th. Moving from the left, a Siberian Cossack Corps under Ataman P. Ivanov-Rinov aimed to hit the 5th Army from the rear. The Whites advanced along a 300-kilometre front and penetrated 350 kilometres deep at the furthest point by 14 October. Delays in the White 2nd Army and the failure of Ivanov-Rinov to get behind the Red

5th prevented full success. Fighting in the centre was particularly heavy, the Reds receiving the worst of it, but they were able to call up an additional 44,000 reserves from the recently-conquered Urals. On 15 October they counter-attacked and within two weeks had pushed the Whites back to their positions at Ishim. Kolchak now had to decide how best to defend the White capital itself.

That autumn, White resistance south of Omsk crumbled. The loss of the railways at Chelyabinsk and Petropavlovsk cut off the southern armies from Kolchak's main forces and completely disrupted their source of supplies. Red forces converging on the Tashkent Railway from the west and the east from Turkestan crushed General Belov's Southern Army in September. Dutov still had 12,000 men on 9 November, but Red forces

Red commander V. I. Chapaev won three St George Crosses as a non-commissioned officer in World War One. He commanded his famous 25th Rifle Division against the Whites on the Volga and Ural Fronts. (Painting by K. D. Kumayka, art card, Voenizdat, 1956)

moved south from Petropavlovsk to Kokchetav, splitting his corps in two. Lacking cavalry, the Reds maintained their momentum by riding in hundreds of carts, 12 men in each, dismounting into firing lines, then loading up and driving on. Half of Dutov's men lacked rifles and ammunition, and a quarter were down with typhus. The Orenburg Army fell apart by the end of November.

The Ural Cossacks also suffered, especially after the British stopped supplying them from the Caspian in August 1919. While engaged at the front, the Cossacks had been unable to bring in the autumn harvest. Cossack and horse now faced starvation. Lacking artillery, shells and ammunition, and stricken with typhus, the Cossacks were pushed back to the town of Kalmykov in late November and then retreated over the Trans-Caspian Desert to Persia.

Five thousand of Dutov's survivors moved south to Semipalatinsk, headquarters of Ataman B. V. Annenkov's 9,000 Semirechie Cossacks. Annenkov's colourfully uniformed Partisan Division was itself in similar straits and nearly surrounded. Losing his capital on 1 December, Annenkov retreated into the Altai Mountains, where, facing starvation,

the division broke into groups and escaped into China.

The Ukraine

On 22 January 1919 the Ukrainian National Republic (UNR) united with the West Ukrainian National Republic (ZUNR). This action was effectively an exercise on paper, as each republic retained its own army and government. The western republic, which had proclaimed its independence in October 1918, immediately clashed with the new, nationalistic Poland. Both claimed the province of Galicia. The western republic's armed forces, the Ukrainian Galician Army

Simon Petliura's Ukrainian army on the march, 1919–1920. By the end of 1918, he had emerged as the leading figure in the Directory Government. In the nightmare of politics that was the Ukraine in those years, Petliura alternately had to fight the Germans, the Poles, the Romanians, Skoropadsky's Ukrainians, the Bolsheviks, Denikin, and Makhno. Poland eventually recognized him as head of the Ukrainian People's Republic in March 1920. Thereafter, Petliura led two Ukrainian divisions in the Russo-Polish War. In October, however, the Poles disarmed his troops, forcing him into exile. A Bolshevik agent assassinated him in the 1920s. (Period art card, Bullock collection)

(UHA), which attained a strength of 70,000 in June 1919, included the elite 1st Brigade of the Ukrainian Sich Rifles which had served in the Austro-Hungarian Army in World War One in the hope of liberating their country from imperial Russia. After hard-fought battles during the first half of 1919, Poland succeeded in defeating the UHA in July. The army then retreated to join the Ukrainian National Republic in the east.

In the meantime, the UNR, led by the Directory, had serious problems of its own. Internally, the UNR was split between political elements desiring to enact a socialist agenda first and the more moderate, including Simon Petlyura, who pushed for national liberation as the primary goal.

The UNR was beset on all sides throughout 1919. To the northwest and southwest the Poles and Romanians wished to round out their borders at the expense of the Ukraine, while peasant revolts, including the most dangerous under the Anarchist Nestor Makhno, were endemic. A Bolshevik-sponsored shadow government, the Ukrainian Soviet Socialist Republic, contested ultimate control, being backed by the Red Army. In February, Red Guards entered Kiev and had pushed the Directory's forces back to Kamenets-Podolsk in the southwest where the UNR resettled.

In the southeast, Denikin's forces entered the Ukraine in June. Petlyura attempted to form an alliance with the Whites, but failed. Denikin considered Petlyura a socialist and had no interest in espousing the cause of Ukrainian nationalism.

However, the arrival of the West Ukrainians allowed for a combined Directory offensive, consisting of 35,000 combat troops, against the Bolsheviks that summer. The UHA reached Kiev on 30 August, the same day as Denikin, but, unwilling to fight the Whites, whom they did not consider enemies, withdrew. The political orientation of the UHA, in fact, was liberal, while the forces of the Directory were largely socialist. These differences spilled over into matters of organization and strategy.

Typhus struck in October, decimating the combined army of the Ukrainian National Republic. Lacking any firm base, low on armaments and beset by enemies on all sides, 2,000 of the soldiers remaining in the field under General M. Tarnavsky decided to join Denikin, while Petlyura retreated with another 2,000 to Poland in December.

The offensive for Petrograd

The White Northern Corps formed in Pskov, Russia, in September 1918. The original 6,000 soldiers, of whom one-quarter were officers, were pushed back into Estonia that autumn by the Red 7th Army. Half of this corps transferred to the Russian-Baltic forces of Prince Lieven at Libau, while the other half served as a detached Russian unit in the Estonian Army under General Johannes Laidoner. The Northern Corps returned to the Pskov Front where they were joined by the mounted Russian partisans of Major-General 'Batko' Bulak-Balakovich in October. Imperial Guards officer General Alexander Rodzianko arrived in February 1919 and took command.

That spring, the Estonian Army expanded to 40,000 and Laidoner succeeded in clearing

Perhaps the only surviving photo of the tank 'White Soldier' in Northwestern Army insignia (see top left). The Russian tricolor chevron is atop a white cross and underneath is the name of the tank in white. This tank's British-trained Russian crew (commanded by Naval Warrant Officer Strakhov) was one of six spearheading Yudenich's assault on Petrograd. (Bullock collection)

Estonian troops in national uniform, two with German helmets, 1919. (Bullock collection)

the Bolsheviks out of his country and northern Latvia. Then, Rodzianko and Laidoner went on the offensive against the 7th Army in May. White and Estonian troops took Gdov, Yamburg and Pskov that month, destroying ten regiments. After the defection of thousands of Red prisoners, Rodzianko's strength reached 25,000. Moreover, 3,100 square kilometres of Russian territory had been liberated, as well as half a million Russians. Now possessing a base, the Northern Corps became independent of Estonia.

General Nikolai Yudenich arrived in June, appointed by the White Supreme Ruler, Admiral Kolchak, to assume command of all White armies in the Baltic region. On 1 July, the Northern Corps became known as the Northwestern Army (NWA).

Yudenich's problems were manifold. The new White territory had been ravaged by war and was in the grips of famine, prompting him to secure economic aid from the American Relief Agency. Militarily, the NWA needed clothes, equipment, munitions and food, and these Yudenich requested from the Allies, particularly from Britain.

Yudenich intended an offensive against Petrograd that autumn and to do so he needed a larger coalition of partners. Several other White armies operated in the Baltic, from Lieven's Corps of 3,000, to the more numerous Western Army (WA) of 15,000–20,000 commanded by Prince Pavel Bermondt-Avalov. Avalov, however, subordinated his army to the German Iron Division and Freikorps formations under General von der Goltz. Above all, the Whites needed the cooperation of Finland, Estonia and Latvia.

None of these countries, however, were in a position to offer substantial aid. Latvia had its hands full with the Germans, and Finland and Estonia naturally desired full recognition of their independence from the Whites before they would commit troops against the Bolsheviks in an offensive war. Yudenich, after prevarication, was inclined to offer that recognition, but Admiral Kolchak refused, preferring to keep the concept of the former Russian Empire intact.

Then, a new offensive by the 7th Army prompted action. Pskov fell in late July, followed by Yamburg on 5 August. Prince Lieven agreed to join Yudenich with 3,000 men. General Marsh, head of the British Military Mission, forced Yudenich to form a government prior to receiving substantial British military assistance. In response, the Northwestern Government, headed by C. G. Lianozov, came into being on 10 August with a liberal agenda meant to appeal to the wider population. This government recognized Estonian independence at last and Estonia agreed to support Yudenich against Petrograd two days later.

Yudenich announced preparation for a renewed offensive on 15 August. British military aid, including uniforms, rifles, artillery, aircraft and tanks, arrived that month in support. Simultaneously, the Royal Navy under Admiral Cowan began serious attacks on the Red fleet at Kronstadt.

According to Western sources, the NWA had between 14,400 and 17,000 troops on 1 September 1919. According to Russian sources the NWA had about 20,000:

14,098 infantry, 345–700 cavalry, 786 machine gunners, 370 communications personnel, 1,345 artillerists, 130 in the armoured train Naval Landing Detachment, 350 in the Tank Battalion, 1,750 troops in reserve, three air detachments of six RE8s, six Mark V tanks, an armoured car detachment under Prince Lieven, four armoured trains and 44–53 pieces of artillery.

These were organized into five divisions with a detached brigade on the right along Lake Pskov (Lake Peipus). The Estonian 2nd Division, the Peipus Flotilla and several armoured trains anchored the far right against the Red 15th Army in the Pskov sector. On the far left, 1,600 Estonian Ingermanlanders intended to attack the fortress of Krasnaia Gorka in conjunction with the Royal Navy. The offensive would be carried out along a 160-kilometre front to a depth of 130–160 kilometres over terrain interspersed with woods, lakes, rivers, streams and sometimes marsh.

Yudenich understood that Kolchak had launched his 'Tobol Offensive' in Siberia and that Denikin's forces had reached Kursk on 20 September, heading for Moscow. Speed just might carry the NWA into that cradle of the revolution, Petrograd itself. The Whites' right flank moved first on 28 September, capturing Luga and severing the railway to Pskov by 5 October. The left flank then pushed from Narva, securing Yamburg on 12 October. The Red 7th Army fell back in disorder. Two days later, the NWA reached Gatchina, 48 kilometres south of Petrograd. Pskov fell to the Estonians on the 15th and by 20 October the NWA took the Pulkovo Heights overlooking the city.

Despite this spectacular advance, several ominous events crippled the gambit. Yudenich had made last-minute appeals to the Finns to attack from the north but General Mannerheim, who was in favour, had been out of office since July. And far from supporting the NWA, Prince Bermondt-Avalov instead turned his Western Army against Riga in Latvia in conjunction with the Germans. Both the Estonians and Royal Navy had to divert assets to deal with this crisis in the south. Still worse, General D. Vemrenko's White 3rd Division failed to cut the vital railway from Tosno to Moscow,

Red Guards await Yudenich's attack on Petrograd,
October 1919. (Painting by V. Serov, Young Guard, 1971)

allowing the Red Army to freely reinforce
Petrograd. On the far left of the line, Krasnaia
Gorka still held against the Estonians.

Against this backdrop, the Red counter-
attack began on 21 October. The 15th Army
struck from Pskov to Luga, threatening the
White right flank and centre. The 7th Army,
now reorganized and reinforced by
thousands of Red Guards raised inside the

Attack on Petrograd

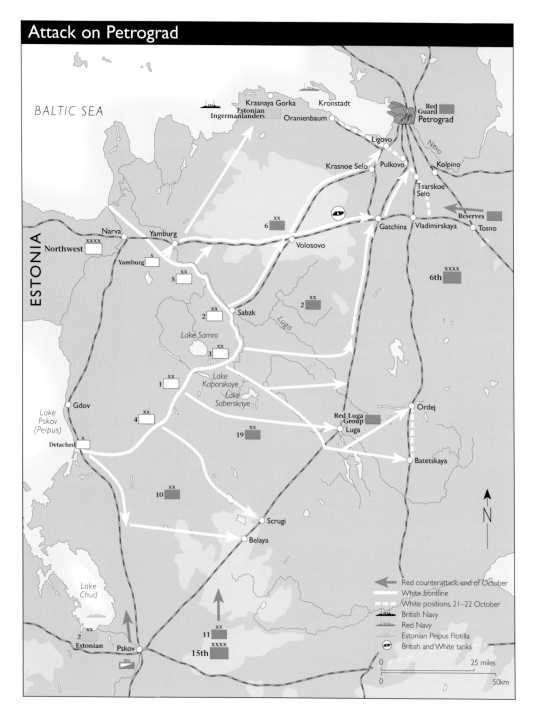

city, pressed westward against the White left and centre. Their combined strength, at least 73,000, forced the NWA back to Gatchina on 3 November, to Gdov on the 7th and to Narva, the starting point, on the 14th.

The NWA, having maintained good order, now found its position untenable. A late autumn cold combined with typhus hit the army hard, claiming several thousand lives. The Estonians, fearing Red reprisals, disarmed and interned the survivors of the

NWA. Sandwiched between a resurgent Red Russia and Germany's territorial designs for the Baltic region, the Estonians signed a treaty with the Bolsheviks on 2 February 1920.

The Armed Forces of South Russia

The Volunteers opened a new offensive, the 'North Caucasian Operation', on 3 January 1919. The Reds had reformed a front with the 11th and newly-raised 12th Armies. These consisted of 150,000 men, of which perhaps only half were combat-ready. Against these, Denikin pitted 25,000, including the cavalry of Wrangel, Prokovsky and Shkuro. At the end of six weeks, in which neither side gave quarter, the Reds broke, yielding 50,000 prisoners and 150 pieces of artillery. This liberated the Terek Cossacks, who sent units to the Volunteer Army and cleared the shore of the western Caspian. White cavalry harried Red survivors northeast into the steppes towards Astrakhan.

The Don Cossacks meanwhile, outnumbered two-to-one and pressed by the Red 8th, 9th and 10th Armies, had fared poorly on their northern and eastern fronts. Morale plummeted, and carefully orchestrated Bolshevik propaganda divided the population against itself: Cossack versus non-Cossack peasant or *inogorodnye*. The withdrawal of their German allies after the armistice additionally left their western flank uncovered at Rostov, Taganrog and in the Donbas. Further, in December 1918, the British made it clear to Krasnov that they would send aid, but to Denikin who had been able to maintain a clear pro-Allied stance.

Therefore, on 8 January, Krasnov bowed to pragmatism and began negotiations to subordinate his command under Denikin into a new organization known as the Armed Forces of South Russia (AFSR). General A. Bogaevsky, a veteran of the Ice March, replaced Krasnov as Ataman of the Don Cossacks on 15 February, and General

V. Sidorin became field commander of the Don Army. Shortly after, Denikin appointed General Wrangel commander of the Caucasian Army and General Mai-Maevsky commander of the Volunteer Army.

The Reds mounted three offensives of varying strength in March, April and May, intending to pin the Don Cossacks in the centre, while crushing their left flank on the Donbas, anchored by the Volunteer Army, and their right flank on the Manych River line, held by the Caucasian Army. The Manych thrust, if successful, would veer southwest towards Rostov, also threatening Novorossisk, effectively splitting the AFSR in two.

Facing north from the White perspective, the Red armies were arranged in an east–west arch: the 14th in the west, 13th, 8th and 9th in the centre and the 10th in the east. These were believed to have a total of 150,000 men while the Whites had only 50,000 in theatre. A further 5,000 Whites were in the Crimea, 5,000 at Odessa and 10,000 were moving north from the Caucasus. A small group of 3,000 defended Russian territory against incursions by the new state of Georgia.

On the left flank, Mai-Maevsky, a former commander of the 1st Guard Corps in World War One, conducted one of the most skilful operations in military history. During these months the 6,000 troops of General A. Kutepov's 1st Corps, consisting of the elite Alexiev, Markov, Drozdovsky and Kornilov Shock Divisions, and attached cavalry, held then defeated 30,000 of the enemy.

Mai-Maevsky's position in the Donets Basin, or Donbas, lay astride an intricate

OPPOSITE Lieutenant General Anton Ivanovich Denikin inspects the Russian Tank Corps in summer 1919 as commander of the Armed Forces of South Russia. Denikin, a highly competent officer who had risen through the ranks due to merit and hard work, was a political moderate. He had established a record for bravery under fire in the Russo-Japanese War and World War One and had among his medals the extremely rare St George Cross with Swords and Diamonds. Experience in World War One included command of the famous 'Iron Division' and the position of chief of staff to the supreme commander in 1917. (Photo, Ullstein Bild)

Russian regulars observe the enemy. Don Cossacks, with red stripes down the trousers, stand to the right. (Russian painting, 1910s)

network of railways that connected key industrial towns such as Yusovka, Debaltsevo, Gorlovka and Rostov. The Volunteers concentrated at rail junctions with supplies and stocks of munitions. A detachment of aircraft carried out reconnaissance overhead, while cavalry and infantry patrolled the ground. Wherever the Reds advanced they were met with a maximum number of Volunteers debouching from troop trains. Armoured trains, which had flanking cavalry troops for protection, offered immediate artillery support while detachments of tanks and armoured cars provided extra punch. The Reds consistently reported being attacked by 50,000 Whites.

The right flank of the AFSR, along the Manych River, became critical in April. The Red 10th Army held the village strongpoint of Velikoknyazheskaya in force with superior artillery. Outflanking them to the north on 17 May, General S. G. Ulagai's cavalry scattered six regiments of B. M. Dumenko's Red Horse. Wrangel meanwhile massed seven cavalry divisions and with one infantry division and supporting artillery made a crude pontoon bridge and crossed the river overnight on 17/18 May. After three days of fighting Wrangel lined up the cavalry as if on parade, complete with bugles and flags, then charged, sabres drawn, conclusively breaking the Red positions and taking 15,000 prisoners. The 10th Army retreated towards Tsaritsyn.

General A. P. Bogaevsky commanded the Partisan Regiment (which later became the elite Alexiev Regiment) during the 'Ice March' or First Kuban Campaign. He succeeded Krasnov as ataman of the Don Cossacks in early 1919, remaining steadfast to the White cause until the final day of evacuation in November 1920. (Deryabin collection)

Meanwhile, the northern *stanitsas* (village communities) of the Don Cossacks, which had been under Bolshevik occupation, had risen again in April. By May, 30,000 Cossacks were in the field behind the Red lines. Denikin now ordered a general advance. Sidorin's Don Cossacks broke through the 8th and 9th Armies, covering 220 kilometres in four days to unite with the rebels in early June and herding the 8th Army towards Voronezh. Mai-Maevsky, reinforced by Shkuro's cavalry, smashed into the 14th Army, moving west to Melitopol while pushing back the 13th Army. The Crimean Whites, General N. Shilling's 3rd Corps, secured the entrances to the peninsula and entered the Tauride, positioning on the lower Dnieper River. The North Caucasian Detachment moved towards Astrakhan while Wrangel advanced towards Tsaritsyn. Also faced with mounting partisan activity in the Ukraine, the entire Red front recoiled.

On the left flank, the AFSR advanced 300 kilometres in June. The 1st Corps, in conjunction with General Toporkov's Terek Cossack Division, captured Kharkov on the 27th after five days' fighting. Simultaneously, Shkuro routed Makhno's partisans who had temporarily joined the 14th Army (previously the 2nd Ukrainian) and took Ekaterinoslav (modern Dnepropetrovsk) on the 29th.

Wrangel's first attempt on Tsaritsyn halted in mid-June against the barbed wire and trench defences of the city. After requesting and receiving detachments of aircraft, tanks and armoured cars, he moved against the city on the Volga on the 29th. The tanks, commanded by British personnel, ripped through the barbed wire, White armoured cars and infantry following and exploiting the breaches, turning the trench lines, while the cavalry dashed through to overrun the city. The Caucasian Army broke the 'Red Verdun' on the 30th. The rich haul included nearly 2,100 train wagons loaded with stores and munitions and, counting the 40-day march up to Tsaritsyn itself, 40,000 prisoners.

The Moscow Directive

Denikin arrived in Tsaritsyn on 2 July. The next day he unfolded his 'Moscow Directive': Mai-Maevsky would advance to Kursk–Orel–Tula–Moscow, the Don Cossacks to Voronezh–Ryazan–Moscow, Wrangel to Saratov–Nizhny Novgorod–Vladimir–Moscow. Later in the campaign the western advance would be amended to include Kiev and Chernigov in the north as well as the capture of Kherson, Nikolaev and Odessa in the south. In the heady atmosphere of those days the Whites accepted the news with enthusiasm. Propaganda trains, posters, armoured trains and flags began to carry the slogan 'To Moscow!'

Wrangel and the Allied military missions were cautiously optimistic, but overall considered the Directive ill-advised. Wrangel himself had espoused two plans in the recent months. The first had been a link-up with Kolchak's forces on the Volga, in effect transferring to that theatre. Denikin sensibly rejected this because the plan would have meant detaching the Volunteers from the Cossacks and exposing their homelands to invasion. Volunteer and Cossack depended on each other for survival.

The second plan involved halting and regrouping, specifically fortifying the flanks at Tsaritsyn and along the Dnieper River, while placing a mobile force in the centre. Behind this protective screen the Whites could conscript and train new armies and could reorganize their rear areas. Their civil administration was in bad shape, often leaderless and full of corruption. The gendarmerie lacked weapons, authority and numbers, making the policing of interior regions almost impossible. The agrarian question had not been solved nor a better way of life created for the populations under White control. These were solid, almost compelling reasons in tune with conventional principles of war.

Denikin argued, however, that the principles of war *in a civil war* had been redefined. Momentum, *élan*, often meant more than numbers. The Whites had proven this often enough in the past. Each month of delay meant more Red reserves in the field, a fact confirmed by White intelligence. In Denikin's view, the acquisition of territory could bring in more recruits even as it magnified the chance that the Reds could collapse internally or face serious insurrections. In any case, with the Red Army in disarray and retreat and an enormous power vacuum extending before him, the lure northward proved irresistible. This lure would bring over half a million square kilometres and 42 million inhabitants under the control of the AFSR.

Despite the Directive, the Whites needed to regroup in July and August. Nevertheless, limited progress continued. In early July, elements of the Caucasian Army shook hands with patrols of the Ural Cossacks under Kolchak just east of the Volga. Wrangel reached Kamyshin on 28 July, moving to within 100 kilometres of Saratov. General Baron Stackleberg's Composite Guard Corps marched into Poltava in the central Ukraine the next day.

The advance into the Ukraine continued in August, with Kherson and Nikolaev falling on the 18th. The Whites' Black Sea Fleet, organized earlier in the year in cooperation with the Allies, sailed to Odessa, landing troops inside the city on the 23rd. Providing covering fire was the pride of the AFSR's navy, the dreadnought *General Alexiev*. Kiev fell on the 30th.

The Reds had also needed to regroup in July. By August they increased their Southern Front to 180,000 and counter-attacked the AFSR in the centre and east. The centre thrust began on 14 August. Directed on Kharkov between the junction of the Volunteer and Don Armies, the Reds penetrated 150 kilometres, reaching Kupiansk ten days later. However, Mai-Maevsky had begun his own limited offensive almost simultaneously with that of the Reds. The Volunteers and Cossacks pinched the salient, and forced the Red Army back to its starting positions by early September.

The Red thrust in the east, commencing on 15 August, proved the more serious.

The Kornilov Shock Division, arguably the finest combat unit of the civil war period. Major General Skoblin (centre) and Lieutenant-Colonel Levitov (to his left). Tall, blonde, handsome, the gallant Levitov displays eight wound stripes on his left sleeve. Skoblin himself sported four. (Hutchinson & Co., 1938)

The 9th and 10th Armies forced Wrangel out of Kamyshin and drove him down the Volga back to Tsaritsyn. From 5 to 8 September both sides grappled over the fate of the city. Fortunately, Wrangel had improved the earlier Red trenches and had a detachment of tanks. Overhead, a flight of British No. 47 Squadron flying Sopwith Camels repeatedly strafed the Red cavalry. Although bled white, the Caucasian Army held, inflicting 18,000 casualties on the Reds.

Meanwhile, the Don Cossacks raised the stakes. On 10 August, General Mamontov with 8,000 troopers of the newly-formed 4th Don Cavalry Corps embarked on a raid in force that cut a circular swathe, 200 kilometres deep, behind the 8th and 13th Armies. Passing through Voronezh and Tambov, the Cossacks dispersed thousands of Red troops, shut down recruiting centres, cut communications, and destroyed or looted storehouses. While at Tambov on 18 August, the corps had nearly captured Trotsky. Mamontov then turned south, re-entering the Don *voisko* in mid-September. Only 20 Cossacks had been lost en route; however, 6,000 returned to their homes to distribute the plunder.

The AFSR then renewed its offensive in September. In the centre, the elite 1st Corps, seemingly unstoppable, entered Kursk on

the 20th and Orel on 13 October. The Kornilov Shock Division took 8,000 prisoners at Orel alone.

The Kornilov Horse (an attached reconnaissance unit) proceeded north to the town of Mstensk. Only the city of Tula, with its enormous armaments factories, barred the road to Moscow, 320 kilometres away.

To their right, Shkuro seized Voronezh on 30 September, the Don Army marching into the city on 6 October. On the left flank, General Yusefovich's 5th Cavalry Corps, which included the old Imperial Guard cavalry regiments, entered Chernigov on the 12th. On the right flank, the Caucasian Army still held Tsaritsyn, and General Erdeli's North Caucasian Detachment of 5,000 blockaded Astrakhan.

Numerically at least, Denikin had seemed justified in his position about the rules of civil war: during these advances the Volunteer Army grew from 26,000 in July to 40,000 in August while the Don Army went from 28,000 in July to 45,000 in August. Overall, the AFSR had increased from

Général du Régiment Drosdowsky – 1919
Capitaine du Régiment Markoff

OPPOSITE General Kutepov's elite 1st Corps, subordinated to General Mai-Maevsky's Volunteer Army, spearheaded the advance on Moscow. A captain of the Markov Division attends 'a general' of the Drozdovsky Division. The general is actually Kutepov himself, who, based on contemporary photographs, variously posed in all the uniforms of 1st Corps infantry. (Allied art card, Bullock collection)

64,000 in May to 160,000 in October. Over 60,000 of these, however, were reserves, in training, or units needed to guard the lines of communications.

These lines of communications became especially vulnerable from late September. On the 26th, the Anarchist partisan leader Nestor Makhno smashed several White units that had been pursuing him at Peregonovka in the Ukraine. Over the next 11 days, Makhno's guerrillas moved 660 kilometres southeast across the Ukraine, ripping their way through the rear of the AFSR. Although no one knew precisely how many partisans there were, Red intelligence estimated their numbers at 25,000.

By mid-October, Makhno had seized Melitopol, Berdiansk and Mariupol, and threatened Denikin's headquarters at Taganrog. At Berdiansk, the Anarchists destroyed a major artillery munitions depot. Ekaterinoslav changed hands three times over the next weeks and remained in Makhno's hands in November.

In order to slow the Anarchists, Denikin transferred a brigade of Don Cossacks and the Terek and Chechen Cavalry Divisions from Shkuro's Cavalry Corps near Voronezh to the Ukraine. These units halted Makhno's incursions and put him on the defensive. A second White force, a 'corps' of infantry under General Slaschev, had to be withdrawn from the AFSR's already overextended front in the west. These units would be sorely missed in the main battle lines in October. In Denikin's own words: 'This revolt had the effect of disorganizing our rear and weakening the front at the most critical period of its existence.'

The Red Army, now reorganized, re-equipped and reinforced, struck back. From 13 to 16 October, Kornilov scouts at Orel had received reports of 'very strong,

dark-haired riders' in 'black leather jackets and trousers', of well-fed soldiers 'clean and in leather jackets' speaking foreign tongues and according to the locals 'not like any Bolsheviks we know'. The languages, in fact, were Latvian and Chinese. Their comrades were in mixed naval uniform and spoke Russian. The first of the communist internationalist shock groups had arrived.

Over the next month the AFSR battled to keep its positions all along the line in some of the most savage fighting of the civil war. Both sides understood the stakes that autumn. The immediate threats were to the left and right of the 1st Corps which had advanced furthest towards Moscow, creating a bulge in the north centre of the line.

In the west, the 14th Army surged forward against the Drozdovsky and the White 5th Cavalry Corps to their left. Two Red shock groups penetrated between the Drozdovsky and Kornilov Divisions, hitting

Lieutenant-General A. G. Shkuro organized and led the 'White Wolves' partisan cavalry in early 1918. In autumn 1918 he commanded the Kuban Cossack Division and from May 1919 a Cossack Cavalry Corps. (Ocherki Russkoi Smuty, 1921–1925)

'Cavalry Attack' by N. S. Samokish, 1922. Red cavalry clash with the Don Cossacks at Voronezh, October 1919. (Soviet art card, c. 1930)

the latter in the left flank and rear. In the centre, the 13th Army struck the Kornilov and Markov Divisions. In the east, S. M. Budenny's Horse Corps (soon renamed the 1st Horse Army or more popularly as the *Konarmiya*) aimed southwest at Voronezh, the railway junction at Kastornoe, and ultimately Kursk. Infantry regiments from the 8th Army supported Budenny's cavalry attack. The depleted cavalry corps of Shkuro and Mamontov braced to counter this threat. At stake was the encirclement of the 1st Corps and the gradual rolling up of the White lines to the east and west.

This issue was decided in the massed battles between White and Red cavalry in October–November on the eastern side of the salient. For the first and most decisive time, White cavalry left the field defeated. Voronezh fell to the Reds on the 24th, followed by Kastornoe the next day, during a blizzard that heralded the onset of winter. Caught between the anvil of Red infantry on the left and the hammer of Red cavalry on the right and almost completely surrounded, the 1st Corps fell back in order, fighting every step of the way to Kursk. The AFSR's gains of 1919 now fell like dominoes.

Red crucible

The retreat of the Germans after the Armistice left a power vacuum across the Bolshevik Western Front. In the name of 'internationalism', not 'imperialism', the Red Army sent small forces against the Baltic states, Lithuania and Belarus, in the first months of 1919. Regardless of word choice, the new nationalist states considered themselves invaded. Working with the Allies, the Germans and the Poles, the new states fought the Reds to an uneasy halt. Throughout the year, the Bolsheviks watched 'communist' disturbances and revolts rock Central and Eastern Europe

and continued to believe the sparks of international revolution would catch alight. Despite such hope, the revolutions in Germany and Hungary collapsed.

The Ukraine proved even more intractable than the Baltic states and Polish-dominated Belarus. In January, the Reds formed the Ukrainian Army Group commanded by Antonov-Ovseenko. By the end of April, most of the Ukraine had been brought under nominal control. But this control proved illusory. Bolshevik policies were heavy-handed and took no note of Ukrainian nationalism. Ataman Grigoriev, after helping the Reds defeat the Allied landings at Odessa and Sevastopol in March and April, next turned on the Reds. Makhno's insurgent army also played havoc with the lines of communication. In the end, Antonov defeated Grigoriev, but not Makhno.

More promising was the state of Trotsky's new model army. In February 1919, the Red Army attained a ration strength of 1 million. By December, that army stood at 3 million. In theory, a Red rifle (infantry) division consisted of three brigades of two regiments each and often component cavalry and artillery. A cavalry (literally *kon*, or 'horse') division contained three brigades of two regiments with component horse artillery. Actual numbers in divisions varied greatly, as it did in the civil war armies of all sides.

The first commander-in-chief of the Red Army was the tough Latvian Ioakim Vatsetis, who assumed that position from September 1918 to July 1919. A former colonel and commander of the elite Latvian Division, Vatsetis had been in charge of the Eastern Army Group in 1918 at Kazan. There, he became associated with Trotsky. S. S. Kamenev, also a former tsarist colonel, assumed command of the Eastern Army Group after Vatsetis in September and would replace him once more on 3 July 1919 when he became commander-in-chief himself.

The White attack on Perm and the destruction of the 3rd Army had taken the Reds by surprise. Stalin and the head of the Cheka, Dzerzhinsky, proceeded to Perm in early January to investigate. The resulting charges included incompetence, lack of centralized command resulting in conflicting orders and lack of discipline, the 2nd Army's failure to support the 3rd Army and the presence of troops in the ranks hostile to Bolshevism. The Red Army obviously had further to go along the path of regularization.

Kolchak's offensive in March also took the Reds by surprise. By subtracting troops

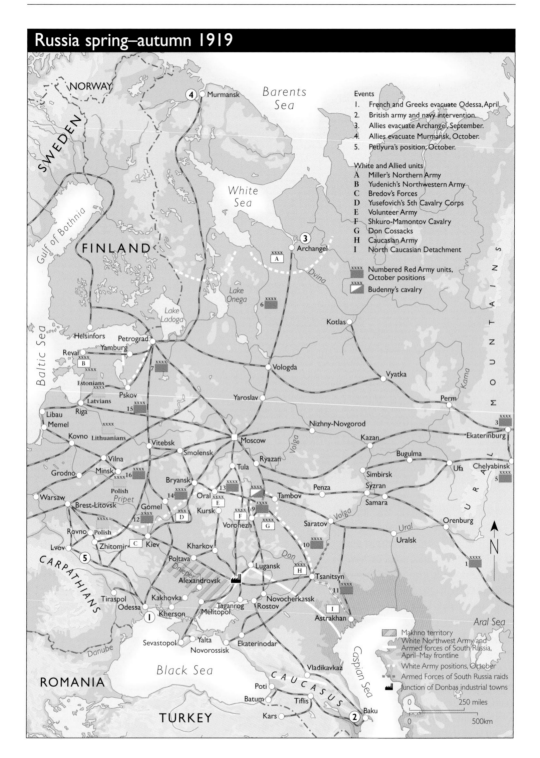

Russia spring–autumn 1919

Events
1. French and Greeks evacuate Odessa, April.
2. British army and navy intervention.
3. Allies evacuate Archangel, September.
4. Allies evacuate Murmansk, October.
5. Petlyura's position, October.

White and Allied units
A   Miller's Northern Army
B   Yudenich's Northwestern Army
C   Bredov's Forces
D   Yusefovich's 5th Cavalry Corps
E   Volunteer Army
F   Shkuro-Mamontov Cavalry
G   Don Cossacks
H   Caucasian Army
I   North Caucasian Detachment

Numbered Red Army units, October positions

Budenny's cavalry

Makhno territory
White Northwest Army and Armed forces of South Russia, April–May frontline
White Army positions, October
Armed Forces of South Russia raids
Junction of Donbas industrial towns

0   250 miles
0   500km

from the Southern Front and drawing on reserves from the interior, however, the Eastern Army Group was able to crest at a ration strength of 361,000 in May, which made a counter-offensive all along the front possible. In conjunction with intense propaganda aimed at Kolchak's levies, Trotsky circulated Order No. 92, forbidding

M.V. Frunze led the (Red) 'Southern Group' against Kolchak from spring 1919 then commanded the Eastern Front in July and August before tackling the Ural and Orenburg Cossacks that autumn. He commanded the Southern Army Group against Wrangel's Whites and the Ukrainians in October 1920. A talented strategist, the prestigious Frunze Military Academy is named after him. (Sovetsky Kudoshnik photo card, Museum of the Revolution)

the shooting of White deserters and prisoners of war. A similar order would be given to the Red soldiers on the Southern and Northwestern Fronts later in the year, during the height of the White offensives. The objective was not compassion for the enemy, but the encouragement of desertion. What happened after White deserters went over and were 'debriefed' by the Red security forces in the rear was another matter.

Kolchak's retreat to the Urals provoked a crisis in the Red high command that summer. Trotsky and Vatsetis ordered Kamenev to hold the Ural line and transfer troops back to the Southern Front to face Denikin. Kamenev, backed by Lenin, wanted to cross the Urals and deliver the death blow to Kolchak. Lenin's position

won out and the pursuit continued. In the end, however, the Eastern Front proved self-sustaining because of the influx of proletarian reinforcements from the Urals factories, so that troops were able to transfer to the south. Indeed, after Kolchak's Tobol Offensive in November, the Red 3rd and 5th Armies had 100,000 to his 55,000, despite the eventual transfer of troops against Denikin.

Lenin moved Stalin to Petrograd in May–June to organize defences in the northwest and appraise the merits of the 7th Army which guarded against the Finns north of the city and the Whites to the west, who had just advanced into Russian territory from their base in Estonia. Contrary to later Soviet mythology, Stalin did perform solid supervisory work and did prepare defences that would be useful later that autumn, but he did not save Petrograd. The Finns were not willing to go to war and the Whites had no intention of advancing on Petrograd at that time. Stalin spent July through to September at Smolensk advising Lenin on the status of the 16th Army on the Polish frontier.

Meanwhile, even as the Reds had had their scare at Petrograd in June, and were wrangling over strategy against Kolchak, they faced a new and more ominous threat from Denikin's AFSR. In January and February, the Reds had pushed their offensive against the Don Cossacks with the 8th, 9th and 10th Armies, while the 11th and 12th Armies of the Caspian-Caucasus Group tried to drive a wedge between them and Denikin's Volunteer Army with a thrust directed on Rostov. The subsequent annihilation of the 11th and 12th Armies by Denikin's forces was the single greatest battlefield loss sustained by any side during the civil war.

Incensed, Trotsky used the debacle to drive home his strictures demanding more professionalism:

These two armies comprised 150,000 or even 200,000 men. At any rate, they indented for supplies for that number. However, these were not properly organized forces, but guerrilla

Russia's future dictator, Josef Vissarionovich Dzhugashvili or 'Stalin' – 'Man of Steel' – on the Southern Front, 1919–20. (Lenfotohudohnik, c. 1930)

detachments, behind which tailed numerous refugees and mere parasites and plunderers. There was no trace of any proper organization of supply, administration or command. Self-appointed commanders were unwilling to take orders from anyone, and fought each other.

Red attempts to regain the initiative in March, April and May were also ground to a halt. Arriving at Kharkov in June, Trotsky described the Southern Front as 'experiencing a grave crisis,' and commented that the 13th Army 'is at present in a state of utter collapse'. His diagnosis of the 8th, 9th and 10th Armies was scarcely better. His culprits were the usual 'guerrilla'-style tactics, misleading and even boastful reports given by subordinate commanders to higher leadership that resulted in a false appreciation of conditions at the front, troops who exhibited, in his words, 'panic, treachery and decay' and commanders who were 'idlers, parasites and traitors'. Draconian methods were adopted to restore order.

Perhaps the main problem at this time was simply the 8,000 kilometres of front lines held by the Reds. Possessing the ability to be decisive on any given front if for no other reason than their larger numbers, they still lacked the strength to be superior everywhere. Then again, the Whites on the Southern Front were of superior quality.

Another attempt to wrest the initiative from the Whites was made in August under the direction of the new commander-in-chief, Kamenev. The 9th and 10th Armies advanced 230 kilometres down the Volga, almost retaking Tsaritsyn before being stopped by the White Caucasian Army. A secondary thrust between the Don Cossacks and the Volunteer Army also failed and the Cossacks launched a massive raid of their own under Mamontov from mid-August to mid-September.

Mamontov's raid focused full attention on the threat from the south and additionally spurred the Reds to form powerful cavalry forces of their own. Trotsky watched the Cossack incursion unfold behind Red lines while situated in his armoured train on the Moscow–Tula line. Previously, he had always considered the cavalry arm to be 'ultra-reactionary' in spirit and inimical to a workers' and peasants' Red Army. By early September, however, he had radically changed his mind. The printing press aboard his train issued orders, disseminated propaganda and published his official newspaper *En Route*. In Circular No. 86 on 4 September, he described the critical situation and plan of action to the commanders on the Southern Front:

Mamontov's men must not be allowed to break through to the north, Tula and Moscow. They must not be allowed to move southward, into the rear of our Red forces on the Voronezh and Kursk sectors of the front. Their routes to west and east must be cut. They are to be exterminated on the spot, to be annihilated like mad dogs.

That week he penned his appreciation of the role of cavalry while at Ryazhsk station, the junction of the Moscow, Voronezh, Tula and Penza rail lines. In *En Route* No. 93, 'Proletarians, To Horse!', he called on the soviets at all locations and command echelons to send cavalry forward for amalgamation into larger formations: 'The Red Army's principal misfortune is its shortage of cavalry. Our war is a war of *manoeuvre* and calls for the maximum mobility.' Demonstrating the extent of his conversion, Trotsky insisted that the 'communist must become a cavalryman'. He ended his famous communiqué with the admonition: 'The Soviet Republic needs cavalry. Red cavalrymen, forward! To horse, proletarians!'

By the end of September, the Reds had rushed every possible reinforcement, every rifle, to the Southern Front. Stalin arrived as Special Commissar to the Southern Army Group on 3 October, commanded by the politically reliable A. I. Egorov from the 11th Army. Stalin and Trotsky both claimed authorship of the plan that ultimately frustrated Denikin's bid for Moscow, but the credit, in fact, belongs to Kamenev. No genius was needed, only a clear-sighted appreciation of the battlefield and a determined application of the principles of war. The White 1st Corps was dangerously overextended and vulnerable on both its east and west flanks. While the 13th Army pinned the 1st Corps' centre in mid-October, the 14th Army with reinforced shock groups drove in from the west.

M. V. Tukachevsky, one of the most brilliant Red commanders alongside Frunze and Blyukher. Despite his background as a former tsarist lieutenant and a minor member of the nobility, the Bolsheviks promoted him into positions of trust. He commanded 1st Army against KOMUCH in 1918, 8th Army against the Don Cossacks in spring 1919, then 5th Army against Kolchak, rising to lead the Caucasus Army Group in early 1920 and the Western Army Group against Poland. He became a Marshal of the Soviet Union in 1935. (Painting by L. Kotliarov, Sovietsky Kudoshnik art card)

Most importantly in terms of morale, the future path of the civil war and subsequent Soviet history was the thrust from the east. Here, Budenny's cavalry, roughly comparable in numbers with the corps of Mamontov and Shkuro, but superior in terms of infantry support, stove in the White flank from Voronezh to Kastornaia. This was the decisive battle, the turning point of the civil war. Writing from his train on 25 October, in *En Route* No. 102 Trotsky proclaimed the simple truth: 'the enemy has been dealt a blow from which he will never recover'.

Focused on Denikin, the Reds were not prepared for the timing and speed of Yudenich's advance on Petrograd on 28 September. Alarmed, Lenin and several of the leading Bolsheviks were in favour of abandoning the city. Trotsky, fresh from the Southern Front, arrived in Petrograd with his armoured train and full staff, effecting what would become his finest days since Kazan. Judging by the flurry and tenor of his orders, however, even he was worried.

Demonstrating an almost immediate grasp of conditions at the front, he castigated the 7th Army units for 'a shameful panic' and 'senseless flight' at Gatchina on the 17th, and for regiments exchanging friendly fire then running away on the 18th. Orders to the 7th Army next described the nature of the enemy and his tactics and what Red commanders must do to counter these. In his own words, the enemy 'always keeps just within range, and by using his machine guns and automatic rifles he develops an impressive firepower which conceals the insignificance of his numbers'. He also derided the persistent cries of being 'flanked' or 'encircled' in reports. 'The enemy operates by night, so as to use darkness to conceal the smallness of his numbers and to frighten us.' And: 'The enemy's interest lies in keeping us at firing distance. … Our interest lies in getting close enough to use the bayonets, when the mere sight of us is bound to overwhelm the enemy's scanty forces.'

Disingenuously, the Bolsheviks had tarred the White Northwestern Army as nothing more than capitalist hirelings. Now they had to deal with reality. Unwittingly, Trotsky's reports had revealed the hollowness of Bolshevik propaganda. Yudenich's men used range and mobility, and fighting in small groups in flank and rear actions at night: in short, the tactics of professionals to lever and hustle a more numerous but less steady foe towards Petrograd.

However, steadiness Trotsky was willing to provide. Order No. 163 stipulated that defeatists were to be 'killed on the spot'. Order No. 165 continued: 'Those who retreat without orders, after being warned, are to be shot on the spot. The battle-police detachments are to bring deserters before the tribunal without delay.' Although an embarrassing and controversial subject to this day, these 'battle-police detachments' represented what White reports identified and described as 'blocking units'. The Red technique of 'blocking' meant that the

Sergei Kirov (born 'Kostrikov') commanded the Red forces at Astrakhan and kept the city out of White hands during the civil war. Later he became a popular mayor of Moscow. His mysterious shooting in 1934 has remained controversial to the present day, but he may have been among the first victims of the Great Purges of the 1930s.

Bolshevik poster by A. Apsit extolling the defence of Petrograd in 1919. (Sovietsky Kudoshnik, 1967)

'battle-police' units machine-gunned friendly forces attempting to retreat before the enemy. Under the circumstances, moving forward seemed the safer option.

At the same time, other stiffening techniques and ploys at propaganda were enacted. To the bourgeois enemy he offered the carrot from his train's printing press, in Circular No. 103: 'Come over to our side. Kill commanders who try to stop you. Come to us! You will be received as brothers.' In answer to the six White tanks advancing with Yudenich that had played havoc with Red morale, Trotsky brought forth tanks of his own. *En Route* No. 99, dated 21 October 1919, proclaimed: 'The first tanks produced in Petrograd have taken part in the fighting,

with undoubted success. The Red troops greeted with delight the appearance of the first armoured caterpillar.' Actually, these 'tanks' were the less fearsome Austin-Kegresse (half-tracked) armoured cars (see Osprey New Vanguard 95: *Armoured Units of the Russian Civil War: Red Army*).

Most convincing, perhaps, was the high state of preparedness of Petrograd itself. Thousands of Red Guards, including women's units, were raised and deployed throughout the city. Petrograd had been made into a 'dreadful labyrinth' of steel and concrete barricades with barbed-wire entanglements that channelled attackers towards carefully prepared machine-gun nests and along avenues where grenades could be tossed from every window. In *En Route* No. 98, Trotsky asked a rhetorical question no less relevant to those experiencing urban warfare in the future: 'every building would be for them either a riddle, or a threat, or a mortal danger. From which direction should they expect the shot to come?'

This particular question would remain unanswered. The combined strength of the 7th and 15th Armies forced the White Northwest Army back to the Estonian border and subsequent internment. What remained for 1920 was the final liquidation of Kolchak and Denikin.

The Black Guards

*'Forward beneath the black flag of Anarchy,
on to the great struggle!'
– poem by Nestor Makhno.*

One of the most remarkable chapters in the history of guerrilla warfare was written in the Ukraine from 1918 to 1921. Here, a part of the larger Anarchist Federation called *Nabat* (Alarm), specifically the military forces of the Makhnovshchina (Makhno Movement), fought all powers in an attempt to establish free soviets and self-governance. The man behind this struggle was 'Batko' (Little Father) Nestor Ivanovich Makhno, a peasant variously vilified as a bandit and monster, or worshipped as a hero.

Extant source documents on the Makhnovshchina are fragmentary. The Bolsheviks destroyed many Anarchist papers and most of the Black Guard leaders were executed or killed in battle. Nevertheless, three accounts from senior commanders survive: those of Peter Arshinov, who was involved from start to finish, those of Nicholas Voline, who served for six months, and Makhno's own.

Nestor Makhno was born in 1889 (some sources state 1888) into a poor peasant family residing in Gulyai-Polye, east-central Ukraine. Implicated in anarchist political activity after the Revolution of 1905, he was sentenced to life imprisonment at the infamous Butyrki penitentiary in Moscow. After serving nearly nine years, most of the time in chains or in solitary confinement in dank cells reserved for the unruly, he was released shortly after the February Revolution of 1917 under the general amnesty granted to political prisoners by the Provisional Government.

At Butyrki he had studied the theory of anarchism under fellow prisoner Peter Arshinov and had given himself a rudimentary education by reading a variety of books, courtesy of the prison library. Although a professed Anarchist, Makhno preferred direct action to theory; indeed, most of his followers understood as little about Anarchist ideology as they did about communism.

According to Russian-American Anarchist Emma Goldman, Makhno's partisans were 'a spontaneous, elemental movement, the peasants' opposition to all governments being the result not of theories but of bitter experience and of instinctive love of liberty. [However], they were fertile ground for Anarchist ideas.'

Based on several eyewitness accounts, Makhno stood just under average height, had piercing grey-blue eyes, long, dark or chestnut hair, a snub nose with a prominent forehead, sometimes had a brown moustache, spoke with a high-pitched voice and was strongly built. Often he was seen with two ammunition belts crossed over his chest and two or more grenades suspended from his vestments, sometimes with a rifle, sometimes with a sabre, and usually with two or more handguns, usually Colt or Nagant revolvers and a Mauser 'broom-handle' automatic. He was considered a crack shot with the handguns and could serve artillery, a skill he required of all his immediate staff. Always a courageous fighter in the front ranks, he survived a dozen wounds.

Makhno himself had no military training. However, he proved himself a brilliant tactician who was able to respond quickly to a multitude of challenging circumstances. Any ruse was acceptable, from using enemy uniforms to feigning retreats or surrender, to moving or attacking in inclement weather.

Speed was a prime ingredient of success, and his army of mobile cavalry, *tachanka* (two- to four-horse machine-gun carts), and

A Makhnovist *tachanka* (centre). Makhno (left display photo). Right display photo depicts Makhnovist cavalry raiding the Berdiansk-Mariupol sector in autumn 1919. The flag, which is a reproduction modelled directly from a period photograph, carries the message of death to those exploiting the labour of working people. (Bullock photo from the Gulyai Polye Historical Museum, Ukraine)

cart-borne infantry could make 100 kilometres a day. Tired horses were exchanged for fresh ones at each village, a system not unlike the American Pony Express a generation earlier. A high ratio of machine guns to soldiers was another prime ingredient. For example, the Makhnovists had a machine gun for every 24 men whereas the Red Army's ratio was one to 67.

On the march, his main column was several kilometres long, with any mobile supply train going first (daily supplies and supplementary munitions), infantry carts and *tachanki* in the centre and the cavalry in the rear – in other words the slowest part of the formation first and not last as was the custom with many armies. Based on descriptions of his battle lines, this was so that the slower wagons could pull up, the carts and *tachanki* could form a defence in the centre, both types of vehicles disgorging troops and positioning the machine guns, while the cavalry could react by coming up on the flanks. This column would seldom be ambushed because cavalry outriders were in the van and rear, and along parallel paths and roads. At night, the carts and *tachanki* made a circle similar to the 16th–17th-century Cossack encampments.

The insurgent army's organization consisted of three battalions to a regiment, three regiments to a brigade and three brigades to a division. These units varied in size with no set number of men being allotted to a particular establishment. Commanders were elected or sometimes appointed by Makhno personally from his trusted clique. All primary commanders came from peasant or working-class stock, most having had experience as non-commissioned officers in World War One. Discipline was swift and harsh and included summary execution by pistol.

In his memoirs, Makhno stated he had 30,000 in his army with arms and another 70,000 that he could draw on when weapons became available. These numbers, however, continually fluctuated. Late in 1918, the combined partisan forces of Makhno and Fyodor Shchuss numbered about 1,500. By 1919, these had swelled to 20,000–40,000. These totals decreased in 1920 to 10,000–15,000 and reached a low point of 1,000–5,000 in 1921. Red Army reports from autumn 1919 estimated the insurgent army at 14,000–40,000 infantry, 6,000–15,000 cavalry and 5,000 gunners and machine gunners. Hardware included 48 field guns, 1,000 machine guns, four armoured cars and four armoured trains.

Konstantin Paustovsky witnessed two of these trains passing through the station at Pomoshnaya in early autumn 1919. On the first, 'I saw young men roaring with laughter, hung all over with weapons – curved sabres, broadswords, naval silver-hilted daggers, rifles, revolvers, cartridge belts. Streaming in the wind, enormous red and black ribbons flew from peaked caps, bowlers and sheepskin hats of every shape and size.' One soldier carried a small black flag with a white sunrise emblem mounted on a lance.

The second train 'carried a magnificent, glossy landau [*sic* – horse carriage] with a prince's gilded coat of arms on the door. From one of its shafts, raised like a flag pole, fluttered a black banner bearing the motto "Anarchy Breeds Order". A machine gun stood at each corner of the wagon, a soldier in an English greatcoat squatting beside it.' Paustovsky then glanced into the 'fierce and vacant' eyes of Batko Makhno himself.

The insurgents, in fact, had many colourful characters: the romantic freebooter Fydor Shchuss; Semyon Karetnik, considered the second best strategist after Makhno and chief of staff; Viktor Belash, a talented organizer, he was chief of staff after Karetnik and the last commander; the final chief of staff, Taranovsky; Tomas Kozhin, commander of the elite *tachanka* machine-gun regiment; Ivan Kartashev, who wrote the 'Ballad of the Makhnovists' to the older tune of 'Stenka Razin'; and Roger 'the Frenchman' who commanded a squadron

'Makhno's Staff on the March' by E. Cheptzov. The flag reads: 'Staff of the Makhnovist Insurgent Army of the Ukraine'. Casimir Teslar reported seeing this same flag flying in Gulyai Poyle in November 1920. Another Anarchist banner read: 'Liberty or Death – the Land to the Peasants, the Factories to the Workers'. The Reds portrayed Makhno's bands as dissolute, drunken hordes. The Anarchists, in return, despised the 'Red Statists'. (Art card, Museum of the Revolution, 1928)

of Belgian armoured cars – given to Russia in World War One – against Denikin in spring 1919.

Some units fighting in the Ukraine pretended to be a part of Makhno's army in order to obtain some measure of political legitimacy, but were only common bandits. Other units, such as the Anarcho-Makhnovist Combat Detachment raised by Comrade Korshun (an alias) in August 1920, formed independently and sought to coordinate their activities with Makhno's main forces. Ossip Tsebry, in his first-hand account, *Memories of a Makhnovist Partisan*, recalled the detachment's winter quarters at Tetiev in 1920–21:

Korshun decided to sit out the winter in the village of Tetiev, which was fortified for the purpose. His fighters were shared around the village homesteads: they were to lend them a hand with the chores and, in the event of the alert being sounded, to muster immediately at an agreed spot to confront the enemy. Thirteen small villages were organized along these lines, each with its own detachment and commander.

Band of Makhno's men led by Fyodor Shchuss (centre). Shchuss wears a Russian Hussar tunic and a sailor's cap. According to eyewitnesses, this cap read (in gold letters) either 'Free Russia', or 'St John of the Golden Tongue'. The latter inscription is borne out in at least one period photo. The tall, long and dark-haired Shchuss was an experienced kickboxer and wrestler who habitually packed a Mauser automatic and Colt revolver along with a Caucasian sabre – and a rifle and two grenades when on campaign. A consummate poseur, this brave and reckless Anarchist wore long boots and heavy spurs as commander of the Cavalry Brigade, while his horse was caparisoned with ribbons and flowers and even 'pearl bracelets' just above the hooves. Shchuss was a notorious Casanova and as late as 2002, locals in the town of Gulyai Polye regaled the author with stories of his local paramours. (Bullock photo from the Gulyai Polye Historical Museum, Ukraine)

Many villages welcomed the arrival of Makhno's forces, either because they had no choice or because a mutually beneficial relationship had been established. These were 'safe zones' where insurgents could return. Booty or commodities could be exchanged for supplies, and medical attention could be secured for the sick and wounded. Based on period accounts, the Makhnovists had telegraph and field telephone operators in these villages so that each could act as a communications centre reporting events, watching enemy movements and coordinating operations. An approaching enemy could be ambushed or the insurgents could retreat, leaving behind an outwardly peaceful Ukrainian village. This system proved resilient. From 1917 to 1921, Makhno's main headquarters at Gulyai-Polye (Field of Pleasure) changed hands 16 times, yet remained a potential 'safe zone'.

The occupation of other villages, however, such as the Mennonite Colonies, was less benign. Makhno had no respect for the prosperous, ethnically German colonists who had been invited into the Russian Empire to improve agriculture and trade in the 18th–19th centuries. Consequently, the several colonies stretching from Alexandrovsk into the Tauride were systematically garrisoned and plundered throughout the civil war period. Gerhard Schroeder's poignant and touching eyewitness account of the repeated sack of one colony, Chortitza, sheds light on the less savoury side of the insurgent movement. Malnutrition and disease followed each occupation, men were routinely beaten and women were violated at will.

Simeon P. Pravda, or 'Batko Pravda' ('Little Father Truth'), commanded the Black Guards at Chortitza. Pravda had lost both legs above the knee in a railway accident, and without the benefit of artificial limbs simply walked on his stumps. A stern disciplinarian, 'Senjka', as he was familiarly known, claimed to have killed 56 men, either with hand weapons or while commanding his *tachanka*. He died in battle in summer 1921 during the liquidation of the Makhnovshchina by the Red Army. Pravda blew out his own brains with a revolver after a wheel of his *tachanka* had broken, rather than be taken alive.

Primarily a rural movement, the Makhnovshchina were less at home in the larger cities. They occupied Ekaterinoslav (currently Dnepropetrovsk) and Alexandrovsk (now Zaporoszhye) in October–November 1919. Despising bank ownership and the role of money, Makhno recognized all currencies, duplicating them at will and overprinting them with a variety of messages – 'the smart money is on Makhno', or, as the author himself witnessed at the Zaporoszhye Historical Museum, 'Hey man, don't be sad, Makhno's got some money now', and, more insidiously, 'Anyone not wanting this money will get his [behind] kicked.'

Although intended as an act of defiance and a 'Robin Hood' gesture to the people, the result was economic uncertainty and inflation. The movement was more adept at distributing propaganda which could find listeners in both town and village. The movement's own newspapers were *The Road to Freedom* and *The Makhnovist Voice*.

Makhno's personal security was always a matter of concern. The Bolsheviks had tried to assassinate him in May 1919 and General Denikin had put a price of half a million roubles on his head that same year. 'The Black Sotnia', a mounted unit of 100–200, acted as his bodyguard. Raised primarily from the Gulyai-Polye area and personally known to each other, they guarded, or fought or commanded partisan bands as needed. At night, Makhno's sleeping quarters were guarded by five to seven men, no one being permitted to come too close while armed. Once, while attending a risky meeting with Petlyura, 20 cavalry went in front and 20 rode behind while Makhno remained in the centre with four *tachanki*. Two shadowy organizations, the Razvedka and the Kommissiya Protivmakhnovskikh Del, acted as an Anarchist equivalent to the Cheka.

As for his opponents, Makhno spoke derisively about Red cavalry, including Budenny's vaunted *Konarmiya*. However, he grudgingly admired the cavalry of the Whites, their ability to change formations quickly, attack immediately and charge with sabres drawn as in the days of old. His battles with General Shkuro's Kuban Cossacks, the notorious 'White Wolves', were particularly savage in June 1919.

Makhno cooperated with the Red Army against Wrangel in autumn 1920, helping break the White Army's lines on the Dnieper and in the Tauride. Next, the Makhnovists were instrumental in forcing the Sivash, which outflanked the White Crimean defences. In appreciation, on 25 November the Bolsheviks surrounded, disarmed and executed thousands of the Black Guards. Another surprise attack struck the insurgents' headquarters at Gulyai-Polye the following day. Over the next months, the Reds methodically liquidated all suspected Anarchists. One by one, battle after battle, in the face of overwhelming odds, the old commanders fell, including Shchuss. On 28 August 1921, the last 83 survivors, including Makhno, made their way across the Dniester River into Romania and internment at Brasov, Transylvania. Refusing Bolshevik demands for his extradition, the Romanians nevertheless encouraged him to move on. Subsequently, the Poles did likewise. Makhno next travelled to France in 1925, a country known for its tolerance of political exiles, and died in Paris in 1935, a broken man.

Allied intervention

Allied intervention can only be understood against the backdrop of World War One. The Bolshevik Revolution of November 1917 removed Russia as a partner of the Allies in the war. Understanding that the Central Powers could now transfer troops from the east to the west, the Allies sought to reconstitute the broken Eastern Front to tie down as many of the enemy as possible. Over the next several months they considered a wide range of partners, from Ukrainians, Serbs, Poles, Romanians, Czechs, to the new players now being called 'Whites' and even the Bolsheviks themselves.

Indeed, each of the Allies believed that the Great War would carry on throughout 1919. They considered it imperative that the Central Powers should not have full access to the munitions stocks and the agricultural and industrial assets still remaining inside the former Russian Empire. Moreover, during the war, the Allies shipped considerable supplies to Russia, some 600,000 tons to the ports of Murmansk and Archangel and considerably more to Vladivostok. These concerns only increased in importance after the Bolsheviks signed the punitive Treaty of Brest-Litovsk, an agreement that placed immense territories under German, Austro-Hungarian and Turkish control.

In retrospect, critics have derided this and related Allied concerns as overreaction. However, at the time there was considerable evidence that what was feared could come to pass. First, the Germans had been responsible for Lenin's return to Russia in 1917. Then, the Bolsheviks staged their first abortive insurrection, the 'July Days', during the height of the Provisional Government's summer offensive. Next, they overthrew that government in November and began efforts to end the war. To the Western Allies, these actions were clear indications that the Bolsheviks were German surrogates in whole or part.

These fears were not allayed when considering the staggering number of enemy prisoners of war, some 450,000, held in lightly guarded Russian camps. Most of these prisoners were Austro-Hungarian, followed by Germans and Turks. For them, repatriation could be as simple as a walk over to the front lines of the Central Powers, a transfer to them as part of a deal, or direct incorporation into units of the potentially hostile Red Army.

Allied representatives, including the Czech Legion, reported that a growing number of prisoners were crowding into cities and rail stations. Indeed, German prisoners had helped bring the Bolsheviks to power in Irkutsk in December 1917 and

Austro-Hungarian prisoner of war confers with Russian captors in Siberia. German and Austro-Hungarian prisoners of war remained a problem for all sides in the civil war. Thousands of a left-wing persuasion joined the Red Guards as 'international' volunteers while a much lesser number joined the Whites. The Allies determined to keep the majority from rejoining the main theatres of war in Europe in 1918. (Russian art card, 1910s)

were confirmed as numbering 2,000 there in early March 1918. A similar number of Hungarians had helped take over Omsk and hundreds of Austrians had been enrolling in the Red Guards in Irkutsk. The fact that several Russians with German-sounding names were signing orders or operating with the Bolsheviks in other locations did not help. For example, Von Rauch, Bauer, Blyukher and many others were logically but incorrectly assumed to be German officers.

By July 1918, the number of 'international' troops in the Red Army had reached at least 40,000–50,000, a sum, however, that included Chinese, Romanians, Poles and extreme-left Czechs as well as Germans and Austro-Hungarians (but not including the Latvian Rifles). Several of these units, for example the 2nd Communist F. Adler Battalion, the Karl Liebknecht Regiment and the Karl Marx Battalion, sounded ominously German. Given the context of the times and the gravity of the strategic situation on the Western Front, the potential threat could not have been ignored by the Allies.

The revolt of the Czech Legion against the Bolsheviks in May 1918 added a new dimension and urgency to these considerations. The Allies now had to establish a new Eastern Front, as well as 'rescue' an ally stuck deep inside Russia. The Legion's spectacular seizure of the Volga and Siberia from May to August effectively forced the Allies to act swiftly.

The Allies in Siberia

Among the major Allied powers, the Japanese and Americans were in the best position to intervene in Siberia. Japan had significant commercial and strategic interests in the Russian Far East and did not have troops committed to a major theatre. The Americans also had important business relations in the Far East, and although they had begun arriving in large numbers on the Western Front, they were relatively fresh to the horrors of war and had troops to spare. The British, French and Italians, though heavily engaged

Vladivostok during the civil war. An American ship floats in the harbour flying the stars and stripes. A small Czech flag is in the forefront. (Czech Legion art card painting, c. 1919–20)

on the Western and Alpine Fronts, were willing to contribute smaller contingents to Siberia as part of the Allied coalition.

The Japanese landed the 12th Division on 3 August 1918 and began operating with the Czechs against Red partisans in the Amur and Assuri regions. Their 14th Division followed, and by November their numbers reached 72,400, under the command of General Otani. All Allied powers in the Russian Far East were to operate under Otani's orders; however, each of the Allies was able to qualify these orders through their own military missions in-country. Following the Russo-Japanese War of 1904–05, Japanese intervention was a sensitive issue. Many Russians, irrespective of political hue, regarded them with suspicion.

The Americans began landing in Vladivostok on 10 August, the 27th Infantry Regiment arriving on the 16th, the 31st Infantry Regiment on the 21st, both regiments and other expeditionary units eventually totalling 7,500 under General William Graves. To the chagrin of the other Allies, however, the Americans and Japanese were not willing to drive west in order to reconstitute the Eastern Front or directly assist the embattled Czechs along the Volga.

For their part, the Japanese refused to venture west of Lake Baikal, securing instead the rail lines, cities and strategic points in

the Russian Far East. For the duration of the civil war, they supplied two Russian commanders with munitions and financing: General Grigory Semenov, Ataman of the Trans-Baikal Cossacks, and General Ivan Kalmykov, Ataman of the Ussuri Cossacks. Later, this support would extend to General Baron von Ungern-Sternberg in Mongolia.

As for the Americans, President Woodrow Wilson decided not to interfere in the internal affairs of Russia beyond securing the railways east of Lake Baikal, providing security and aid for the Russian people, and ensuring the Czechs could evacuate safely to the Western Front. These views were communicated directly in a presidential memorandum given to Newton Baker, Secretary for War, for personal delivery to General Graves. Although the State Department favoured a stronger action to re-form an Eastern Front and stymie the Bolsheviks, the War Department's strategy of sending all possible troops to the Western Front prevailed.

Throughout the Siberian intervention, Graves interpreted these instructions to the letter and remained strictly neutral towards the various Russian factions. This position increasingly drove the British and French, and even the American proponents of a more vigorous intervention, to distraction. Graves, in fact, immediately found himself in an economic, political and strategic rivalry

American, Japanese and Allied officers in eastern Siberia. The back has handwriting in German: 'American and Japanese officers, our guard troops in Krasnaya Retchka'. Krasnaya Retchka was a prisoner-of-war camp incarcerating 2,000 Germans captured in World War One, 1,500 of them officers. Company E, of the American 27th Infantry Regiment, took control of the camp's brick garrison buildings in November 1918 and brought in badly-needed medical and food supplies. The commander of Company E was Captain Ed Larkins, who is probably the captain seated in the centre. Several hundred thousand German and Austrian prisoners were still in Russia awaiting repatriation to their homelands during the Russian Civil War. (Bullock collection)

with the Japanese and with their warlord puppets Semenov and Kalmykov, whom he came to detest. By 1919, Graves had formed a negative impression of the entire White cause in Siberia. Not surprisingly, the Whites looked on American intervention as at best neutral and at worst hostile.

The British landed 543 men of the 25th Battalion, Middlesex Regiment, in July 1918. Over the next weeks the British fought alongside a White Russian unit under Kalmykov and a Czech battalion against Red partisans on the Ussuri. Then they proceeded to Omsk in western Siberia, leaving a few garrisons at strategic points along the rail lines. The British commander, Colonel John Ward, toured the Urals, inspecting KOMUCH and Czech positions at the front. The 9th Battalion, Royal Hampshire Regiment, arrived in October and also travelled to Omsk. These and other smaller units, totalling approximately 1,400 men, remained in close contact with the head of the British Military Mission, General Sir Alfred Knox. Knox, an outright supporter of Kolchak and a clear enemy of the Bolsheviks, was perhaps the most experienced and brilliant figure among the Allies in Siberia. Under his direction, the British took the foremost hand in the supplying and training of Kolchak's forces. Consequently, the Whites respected Britain above the other Allies.

Following a request by the British, the Canadian Siberian Expeditionary Force, consisting of the 16th Brigade (259th and 260th Battalions with smaller technical and support units), began arriving in Vladivostok on 26 October 1918. General J. Elmsley commanded the 5,000 men earmarked for intervention. However, because of the Armistice and a prompt reversal of policy by the Canadian government, only 3,800 actually arrived. These were evacuated on 5 June 1919. Interestingly, the 1st Canadian Tank Battalion volunteered for service in Siberia but the unit never arrived.

The French appointed General Maurice Janin head of their military mission and placed him in charge of the Allied forces in western Siberia. However, Kolchak negated much of Janin's influence by refusing to place Russians in Russia under direct French command. The French themselves contributed 1,076 troops in the summer of 1918. These included an Indo-Chinese battalion, an artillery battery and a reinforced company of volunteers from Alsace-Lorraine. After fighting on the Ussuri, these proceeded to the Ural Front, seeing action at Ufa and Chelyabinsk in October–November. French aircraft with instructors earmarked for the Whites arrived in spring 1919, as did tank personnel who provided training on machine guns. The tanks themselves only arrived briefly at Vladivostok during the French evacuation on 28 April 1920.

France additionally organized units among foreign nationals, former prisoners of war and

Americans stand beside Ataman Kalmykov's armoured train in eastern Siberia, 1918–19. One of Kalmykov's soldiers peers from the observation tower. For details on this armoured train see: New Vanguard 83, *Armored Units of the Russian Civil War: White and Allied*.

Two American infantry regiments transferred from their bases in the Philippines to Siberia, the 27th and the 31st. The 27th arrived in Vladivostok on 16 August 1918, the 31st following five days later. Both regiments earned their nicknames in Siberia. The 27th became known as the 'Wolfhounds' due to a Japanese dispatch that compared their rapid rate of marching to that of 'Russian Wolfhounds' (the borzoi breed of dog). The 31st subsequently became known as 'The Polar Bear Regiment' (not to be confused with the American 339th Infantry Regiment known as 'The Polar Bears'). The 27th evacuated Vladivostok between January and March 1920 and the 31st followed in April. (Bullock collection)

soldiers who previously had served the tsar or Provisional Government. The French formed a Polish Division of 12,000 that saw action along the rails in central Siberia from late spring 1919, a regiment of Serbs at Chelyabinsk and another at Tomsk combined with Slovenes and Croatians, these two units totalling 4,000. President M. Masaryk of the Czechoslovak National Council permitted the French to directly incorporate the Czech Legion into the French Army for the duration of the war. The French Military Mission recorded their number at over 60,000.

Other members of the Allied coalition included China and Italy. The Italians

The 9th Battalion, Royal Hampshire Regiment, transferred from India to Vladivostok in October 1918. The Hampshires crossed Siberia to Omsk, Kolchak's capital, before departing for England in November 1919. Here, soldiers stand beside a 'submerging boat' or semi-submarine, an experiment by Russian Lieutenant Botkin and a relic of the Russo-Japanese War, on display in Vladivostok. (Royal Hampshire Regiment Museum)

contributed at least 1,400 men and established these in garrisons from Vladivostok to Krasnoyarsk. China continued to guard and administer the Chinese Eastern Railway in Manchuria alongside the Russians in accordance with an earlier treaty.

The Allies confined themselves to restoring order over the thousands of miles of Russian railways, garrisoning fixed points and fighting Red partisans, who by all accounts numbered between 80,000 and 100,000. Most encounters with the partisans involved skirmishes between dozens or hundreds of men, but sometimes a few thousand. Only on the Amur and Ussuri Fronts in 1918 did they face down Red formations of 10,000–18,000 in pitched battles.

From March 1919, the Inter-Allied Committee, consisting of representatives from each of the Allied powers with a Russian as chairman, controlled the railways and through their subordinate boards supervised maintenance. American engineer John Stevens headed the Technical Board, a body of 300 experts from the United States. Originally invited to improve the rail system by Kerensky and known as the Russian Railway Service Corps, the team did not arrive in Siberia until March 1918.

Theoretically, Bolsheviks, bandits or hostile elements were not to be allowed within ten kilometres of the railways, a guideline to be enforced by the Allied military troops on hand that guarded specific sectors of the lines. In general, Allied administration of the considerable supplies flowing westward to Kolchak was as honest as the administration of the railways was competent. However, given the dilapidated state of the Russian railways, the competing interests of the Allies themselves, the 'carrying charges' exacted by White warlords like Semenov and Kalmykov, and predatory raids by partisans, much less reached the front than had been sent out.

From start to finish, internecine squabbles crippled the effectiveness of the Allied coalition. Each ally brought its own national goals to the table, none could agree with another on a common strategy and none but the Japanese possessed a sufficient number of troops for decisive action. If any one or two of

The Czechoslovak Legion guarded the Trans-Siberian Railway from 1918 to 1920. In 1919–20 their primary duty was along the lines of communications fighting Red partisans. (Painting by Jindrich Vlcek, art card, 1925)

the powers had been willing or able to commit a few brigades to shore up Kolchak's untried levies, the outcome on the Volga–Urals Front in 1919 would have been quite different.

In the end, most British formations evacuated Siberia by November 1919 and the Americans by April 1920. Most of the other Allies evacuated between these dates, the last echelon of the Czech Legion embarking in August 1920. The last of the Allies, the Japanese, departed on 20 October 1922.

The Finnish Civil War and intervention in North Russia

All of the reasons supporting Allied intervention in general were valid for the landings in northern Russia at Murmansk and Archangel. In addition, the Allies were concerned that the Germans might seize the ports of Murmansk and nearby Petchenga and use them as bases for the U-boats that were wreaking havoc on Allied shipping in 1918. Moreover, the ports of Murmansk and Archangel were possible points of evacuation for the embattled Czech Legion. These concerns were not unfounded, thanks to recent events in Finland.

For much of their history, the Finns had been dominated by either Sweden or Russia. Finland had been a part of the Russian Empire since the end of the Russo-Swedish War of 1808–09. The February and October Revolutions in 1917 revived Finnish hopes for a nation free of either Swedish or Russian influence. Two politico-military factions arose during the course of 1917, the 'Civil Guards' or 'Whites', and the 'Workers' Security Guards' or 'Reds'. The collapse of Kerensky's Provisional Government in November emboldened the Finns, under their future head of state, Pehr Swinhufvud, to declare independence on 6 December 1917.

This new country lacked established military and security forces; consequently, real power lay in the hands of the paramilitary groups, whether Red Guard or White Guard. Each of these factions, however, projected a different and irreconcilable socio-economic vision for Finland. Recognizing the need for a more regular army, the fledgling Senate backed the White Guards, creating the 'Finnish White Army' on 15 January 1918 and naming General Baron Carl Mannerheim commander.

The first serious clashes between White and Red occurred from 17 to 20 January in Karelia. Then, on the 26th, the Finnish Red Guards declared revolution and appealed to Lenin for support. The Russian Bolsheviks, however, were never able to maintain more

than 10,000 men in the field in support of the Red Finns. The Whites, on the other hand, requested support from imperial Germany.

Over the next months, the number of troops on each side fluctuated between 50,000 and 90,000. The Whites possessed three formidable units which were instrumental in their eventual victory: the elite, German-trained Finnish Jaegers, numbering 2,000; the 10,000-strong German Baltic Sea Division under General Baron Rudiger von der Goltz that intervened in March; and the German Brandenstein Detachment of 3,000 that landed in April. The Whites celebrated victory in Helsinki on 16 May 1918, and, as a matter of course, Finland remained under German influence until the Armistice in November.

Finland's disposition affected the Allied contingents allotted to Murmansk and Archangel because a hostile force could drive east through Russian Karelia, cutting the Murmansk–Petrograd Railway. This would prevent any Allied move south and bottle the Allies up at Murmansk. Further, an enemy positioned on the railway at Kem or Kandalaksha (240 kilometres) would sever the one overland road – in reality more of a reindeer track – that haphazardly connected Murmansk to Archangel.

Climate also played a part in every Allied plan. While Murmansk remained relatively ice-free throughout the year, the port of Archangel froze solid between November and April. This affected the timing of Allied intervention, the reinforcement and supply schedules and even the moment of final evacuation.

Intervention proceeded at Murmansk in stages, 500 British Royal Marines landing in March and May. 'Syren Force', a body of 600 troops under British Major-General C. M. Maynard, arrived on 23 June. These groups linked up with a battalion of Serbs that had marched north from Odessa. Then, an Italian contingent landed on 3 September. By the end of 1918, 6,832 British and Canadians, 1,251 Italians, 1,220 Serbs, 731 French and 4,441 locally raised troops (including Russians of the Karelian Regiment and Finns of the

Major-General Sir C. M. Maynard commanded the 'Murmansk Force' dispatched from England to Murmansk, North Russia, in June 1918. Enlisted members wore a white star on a midnight blue patch (symbolizing the North Star) on the right shoulder. Maynard himself wore the same insignia, but as an armband on the right arm. (Provenance unknown, damaged photo, c. 1918)

Finnish Legion) were on the Murmansk Front. The Finnish Legion consisted of pro-Bolshevik elements that had been pushed out of Finland during their civil war.

Through to the end of October, Maynard engaged in several battles in central Karelia that pitted his British-led 'Red' Finns against German-led 'White' Finns. Ironically, Maynard had to fight these low-intensity engagements in the forested marshes while being unsure if his Finnish Legion might turn on him. The local soviet administration at Murmansk eventually decided to declare for the Allies but the question of a Bolshevik invasion into the north from Petrograd made Allied security problematical. Indeed, Maynard had already turned back one such incursion at Kem at the

end of June. In July, he took up defensive positions to the south at Soroka.

The Allies bound for Archangel, the 'Elope Force' under British Major-General F. Poole, initially landed at Murmansk in late June 1918. Poole's original 500 men were reinforced by French, Polish and additional marines on 30 July. Poole himself had arrived at Murmansk in May and had acted as overall coordinator of both Syren and Elope forces prior to a future landing at Archangel.

Encouraged that Allied intervention was imminent at Archangel, local White Russians revolted and seized the port, facilitating Allied entry on 2 August. The American contingent, comprising the 339th Infantry Regiment, the 310th Engineers and smaller supporting units under the command of Colonel George Stewart, arrived on 5 September. By the end of 1918, the Allies at Archangel consisted of 6,293 British and Canadians, 5,302 Americans, 1,686 French, 2,715 Russians (including 500 of the 'Slavo-British Legion') and 300 men of the Polish Legion.

North Russia 1918–20

BARENTS SEA

Whites [ ]
Murmansk Allies [ ]
① ④

FINLAND

KOLA PENINSULAR

Kandalaksha

Finnish
Forces [ ]

WHITE
SEA

Kem

Soroka

German
Forces [ ]

Undozero

Karelian
Nationalists [ ]

Medvejya Gora

Povynetz

Shunga
Shunga
Peninsula

Sordavala

Petrozavodsk

Lake
Onega

7th [ ]
xxxx

Lake
Ladoga

▶ to Petrograd

Sumski Posad

Onega

Obozerskaya

Bolshiozerki

Emptsa

Plesetskaya

Onega

6th [ ]
xxxx

▼ to Vologda

to Vologda

Allies [ ]
Northern
Army [ ]
xxxx Archangel
② ③

Pinega

Mezen

Pinega

Emetskoe

Seletskoe

Dvina

Bereznik

Tarasova

Tulgas

Shenkursk

Velsk

Vaga

6th [ ]
xxxx
Kotlas

N ▲

1. Allies land April 1918 and eventually
    evacuate in October 1919.
2. Allies land August 1918 and evacuate
    in September 1919.
3. Whites forces in the region collapse
    in February 1920.
4. Whites forces in the region collapse
    in March 1920.
⟵ Red advance 1920
      Allied/White positions, October 1918
─ ─ ─ Allied/White positions, September 1919

0   100 miles
0   200km

Nicholas Chaikovsky, a Socialist
Revolutionary, headed the Russian Northern
Government at Archangel in August, a post
he would hold until January 1919, when
P. J. Zubov succeeded him. Originally,
Colonel B. A. Durov served as
governor-general of the northern region.
General Marushevsky succeeded him in
November and was replaced in turn in
January 1919 by General E. K. Miller,
who held the additional title of
commander-in-chief of White forces
at Archangel and Murmansk.

Poole's challenge from August through
to September had been to create a defensive
perimeter around Archangel before the onset
of winter. Poole determined to extend Allied
positions to the south, while securing both

flanks, and holding open the possibility of linking up with loyal Russian forces to the east in Siberia. Additionally, within this new enclave, local Russians could be recruited as part of a new northern White army.

To these ends, Poole advanced five columns. The first and most important, the 'Railway Column', extended southwards along the rail line past Emptsa to just north of the strategic railway station of Plesetskaya. This thrust aimed at the city of Vologda. Two ancillary columns protected this advance, a garrison at the town of Onega and a covering force at Emptsa.

The second most important column, the 'Dvina Column', secured positions at the confluence of the Vaga and Dvina Rivers near Bereznik. This column then captured Tulgas on the Dvina and Shenkursk on the Vaga (340 kilometres from Archangel), and after extending defensive perimeters outwards, proceeded to dig in. The Dvina Column held open the possibility of reaching the city of Kotlas (640 kilometres from Archangel) in spring 1919, which was connected by 320 kilometres of rail to Viatka, which itself connected to Siberia. The final column garrisoned the town of Pinega, 160 kilometres east of Archangel.

Major-General Edmund Ironside replaced Poole as commander of Elope Force in October. From November, the Bolsheviks directed counter-attacks, delivered by the 6th Army, against the Allied columns. Initially, the Reds had a superior advantage in heavy artillery as well as in gunboats, a flotilla of riverine craft operating out of Kotlas. British intelligence estimated the 6th Army at 20,500 men in January 1919, up from 9,000 the previous September.

The Armistice removed the primary reasons for Allied intervention in the north. Yet evacuation could now not occur until late spring or summer 1919 because of the onset of winter. Already, the White Sea had begun freezing, preventing the evacuation of Archangel, and the Allies on the Murmansk Front could not exit and leave the forces at Archangel unsupported.

The winter of 1918–19 caused incredible hardships: supplies had to be brought up by

Meeting of the Allies at Verst 455, Vologda Front, North Russia, 5 May 1919. American Colonel George E. Stewart (left) salutes American General Wilds B. Richardson (right). Stewart commanded the 339th Infantry Regiment, nicknamed 'The Polar Bears'. White Russian soldiers attend the rail gun (centre) whilst British personnel stand atop the troop train (far right). (US Signal Corps)

sledges pulled by reindeer or sleds pulled by dogs, weapons froze, as did exposed flesh, and in the skies a seemingly endless 20 hours a day of darkness reigned. Troops sheltered in villages or in log blockhouses ringed by barbed wire. In January 1919, the Reds forced the Americans, Canadians and White Russians out of Shenkursk, the most exposed salient, but the Tulgas positions held.

Meanwhile, the Allies and General Miller concentrated on building a reliable White army that could stand against an anticipated Bolshevik invasion of the north. This army grew steadily. In January 1919 Miller possessed 6,000 men, by February 12,000, by April 16,000 and by autumn he attained a ration strength of 50,000.

This expansion was not without danger, due to the intense Bolshevik propaganda directed against the White recruits. In April a battalion of the 3rd Northern Rifle Regiment mutinied, while in July Dyer's Battalion of the Slavo-British Legion rebelled and the 5th Russian Infantry Regiment garrisoning Onega handed over that town and the immediate sector to the Reds. Other revolts took place that month in the 6th and 7th Russian Infantry Regiments. These disturbances underscored the basic unreliability of many of Miller's soldiers. In fairness to the Whites, almost every one of the Allies at one point had to deal with instances of insubordination and mutiny.

One hopeful event occurred on 21 March 1919 when a Russian patrol under Captain Alashev made contact with General R. Gaida's White Siberian forces at the village of Ustkozhva. But a meaningful union of armies was not to be. By the end of summer, when sufficient Allied forces were on hand, Admiral Kolchak's Siberians had already begun their long retreat.

Having decided to withdraw from intervention in North Russia before the winter of 1919–20, the Allies began final operations that could give the Whites a chance to survive.

On the Murmansk Front, General Maynard took Sumsky Posad in February, which opened up at least a precarious land route to Archangel. In April, he disbanded the now-unreliable 'Red' Finnish Legion. Also that month, the Allies and White units, including the Russian Rifle Regiment and the Olonetz Regiment, moved south along the railway to Lakes Undozero and Urosozero and from there 80 kilometres further south to Medvyejya Gora. Here, situated on Lake Onega, the Allies constructed a seaplane and armed motor-boat base and began training the Whites in their use.

This additional territory produced more recruits, so that by August, White strength reached 7,000. Already, however, the Allies had started evacuation: the French in June, the American railway troops in July and the Italians and Canadians in August. In August, Maynard and Russian troops under General Skobelitsin attacked Red positions on the Shunga peninsula. The Whites were left in positions along the northern shore of Lake Onega as the last of the Allies withdrew from the Murmansk theatre on 12 October.

At Archangel, two brigades of British volunteers arrived in May and June as a covering force for the eventual Allied withdrawal. The first, under Brigadier-General G. Grogan, struck the Red Army on the Dvina Front in June. The second, under Brigadier-General L. Sadleir-Jackson, hit the 6th Army on the Dvina River in August, putting six Red battalions out of action and taking 3,000 prisoners. General Miller's Russians then took over the front lines.

Germans inspect a Russian Renault armoured car captured from the Bolsheviks in Latvia, 1918. (Photo, Bullock collection)

The Americans and Canadians had already evacuated the Archangel Front in June and the last of the Allies left on 27 September. General Miller's Whites fought on that autumn, but after the retreat of Yudenich and Kolchak, the Reds were free to reinforce the north. Many of the White regiments in the Murmansk theatre were surrounded and annihilated, Murmansk itself falling on 21 February 1920. Archangel had fallen two days earlier, the last of the Whites who were able to, including Miller, escaping by icebreaker into exile. White officers and politicians who had not escaped were shot en masse by the Bolsheviks.

The Baltic

The British took the lead in intervening in the Baltic from 1918 to 1920 due to the geographic proximity of these countries and the ready availability of the Royal Navy. Estonia, Latvia and Lithuania had been quick to seek independence from Russia in 1917. Latvia declared independence on 12 January 1918, followed by Lithuania on 16 February and Estonia on 24 February. Actual independence was problematical, however. The Germans had occupied Lithuania in 1915 and had taken over Estonia and Latvia in February 1918. The ensuing Treaty of Brest-Litovsk, signed by the Bolsheviks and the Central Powers on 3 March 1918, theoretically ended World War One on the Eastern Front. Unfortunately for the aspirations of the Baltic states, the Germans remained in control until the Armistice ending World War One itself on 11 November 1918.

The terms of this armistice required substantial German forces to remain in the Baltic as a hedge against Bolshevik expansion until released from such duty by the Allies. These conditions suited German politicians and adventurers who wished to annex the Baltic region to the new Weimar Republic, but they were unpalatable to the majority of troops who only wished to go home. The Baltic states themselves were divided internally between those who favoured cooperation with the Germans, those who sought full independence with recognition and support from the Allies, and those who desired revolution and alliance with the Bolsheviks.

In late November 1918, the Estonian National Council, which had not yet had time to establish a fully-functioning government, asked for British troops and

The Kuperjanov Partisans were one of Estonia's elite battalions. The patch on the left sleeve is black, bordered white, with skull and crossbones in silver. The cockade is silver with the Estonian tricolor (from bottom to top) white-black-blue. (Bullock collection)

warships in order to deter an invasion by the Red Army. In response, Britain sent munitions and ships of the Royal Navy, but no ground forces. In December, the Reds began to invade Estonia and Latvia with their 7th Army, aided by internal Bolshevik insurrections. The Germans reorganized their forces, the most reliable elements and volunteers being placed under the command of Major-General Rudiger von der Goltz.

The British faced several daunting challenges. Rear Admiral Walter Cowan took charge of naval operations in January 1919 and a full military mission arrived in Estonia under Lieutenant-General Sir Hubert Gough in May. Gough had to assist the new Baltic nations on their road to independence while using slender British resources to control the Germans in accordance with their treaty obligations. This meant holding back the spread of Bolshevism into Europe while thwarting the Germans in their real intentions to create a territorial enclave in the Baltic. Additionally, he had to nurture the small but growing force of White Russians under General A. P. Rodzianko that had formed in Estonia to fight the Bolsheviks.

In all, Cowan variously commanded 238 ships in 1919, including two Italian, 14 American and 26 French. Understanding that he would have to neutralize the Red Baltic Sea Fleet, Cowan established an advance naval base at Biorko Sound on the Finnish coast. With the Germans gone, Finland, led by its regent, General Mannerheim, cooperated with the Allies. From Biorko, Cowan duelled with the Red fleet based at Kronstadt, a fortified island in the bay of Petrograd that was protected by minefields.

In June 1919, Lieutenant Augustus Agar used his section of 40-foot coastal motor-boats (CMBs) to sink the Red cruiser *Oleg*. The first aerial attacks on Kronstadt from Cowan's seaplanes, launched from the carrier HMS *Vindictive*, began on 30 July. Then, on the night of 17/18 August, the seaplanes attacked, distracting enemy gun and anti-aircraft fire while Agar's CMBs, skimming over the minefields thanks to

their shallow draught, slipped into Kronstadt. The CMBs launched torpedoes point-blank into several Red ships, sinking the battleships *Petropavlovsk* and *Andrei Pervozvanni* and the troop ship *Pamyat Azova*.

The British subsequently supported General Yudenich's White Russian advance on Petrograd in autumn 1919. They also tried, but failed, to coordinate a larger offensive using all White forces in the Baltic in unison with the Finns, Estonians and Latvians. In the end, the British Military Mission did provide meaningful political and material support to the eventual independence of Estonia, Latvia and Lithuania.

The Allies in South Russia

In December 1917, Britain and France had agreed to divide spheres of interest and potential economic gain in southern Russia: France taking the grain-rich Ukraine, including the Crimea and Donets industrial basin, and Britain the eastern ports of the Black Sea including the oil-rich Caucasus and Caspian. The collapse of the Central Powers on the Balkan Front in November 1918 encouraged the French to intervene by shifting forces from that theatre to South Russia. France's grand design for the post-war world was to create a *cordon sanitaire* from Riga to Odessa, a security belt of states as a hedge against Bolshevism on the one hand, and against a German national resurgence on the other. Further, France decided to encourage local armies to fight the Bolsheviks.

To these ends, the French landed troops at Odessa on 18 December 1918 and Sevastopol on 25 December. General Philippe d'Anselme arrived to assume overall command on 11 January 1919. The Greeks also decided to intervene with France, having been one of the Allies in World War One. Greece sought to protect a considerable ethnic Greek population in the southern Ukraine as well as gain a larger voice in the post-war political arena. Consequently, the Greeks began landing their troops at Odessa on 20 January.

Originally, French plans had encompassed a sizeable force of 20 Allied divisions, but quickly whittled this number down to 12, then to six, and, in the end, only five arrived. The French expedition included the 30th and 156th Infantry Divisions and the 16th Colonial Infantry Division while the Greek force consisted of the 2nd and 13th Infantry Divisions. Both nations additionally sent supporting troops and several ships.

These units numbered approximately 40,000, or 50,000 if local Ukrainian and Russian forces that occasionally fought alongside the Allies are included. More impressive on paper than reality, the Allies were seriously under-strength. Many of the French had been stricken with the deadly Spanish influenza virus in the Balkans, while the Greeks found it difficult to transport, supply and finance their expeditionary troops in the field. Above all, most of the Allied soldiers simply wanted to demobilize, and several mutinies aboard ship and in the field ensued as a consequence.

Over the next weeks the French and Greeks expanded their bridgeheads at Odessa and Sevastopol. The French occupied Tiraspol on 7 February, the Greeks and French fought their way into Kherson on 29 February and the Greeks entered Nikolaev on 2 March.

The advance to Tiraspol had brought the French and Greeks into contact with another of the Allied powers, Romania. The Romanians had occupied the Russian province of Bessarabia after the Bolshevik Revolution and had established their own bridgehead across the Dniester River. Most Romanian attention, however, was focused on extending their territory to the west in Transylvania and defending Bessarabia against sundry bands of Ukrainian guerrillas. Thus Romania could only anchor the left flank of the Allies.

From the start, the Allies failed to achieve unity or a political consensus. Russian troops loyal to General Denikin's AFSR refused to go directly under French command. Ukrainian forces under General Petlyura desired freedom from both Allied control and domination by the Whites. Moreover,

Bolshevik agitators subjected the inhabitants of the occupied zones to an intense campaign of propaganda. Consequently, the quality and quantity of forces raised locally by the Allies were not impressive.

Having overstretched their positions and having failed to rally significant numbers of the population, the Allies were then attacked by elements of the Red Army. The largest resistance came from Anatoli Skachko's 'Forces Group Kharkov', which numbered about 40,000 by March, a number that does not include the thousands of irregular forces loosely allied with the Reds. Skachko's troops were a collection of proletarian volunteers, hastily conscripted peasants and former soldiers, and bands of partisans commanded by colourful chieftains such as Ataman Grigoriev.

This horde reorganized several times, two main groups hiving off to capture separate objectives – the 'Forces Group Odessa' striking southwest towards Kherson, Nilolaev, Berezovka and finally Odessa, while the 'Forces Group Crimea' headed south towards Sevastopol. Mobile and living off the land, the Reds held the initiative and were able to attack Allied fixed points in turn. Kherson fell on 10 March and Nikolaev four days later. On 18 March, French, Greek and Russian forces were defeated at the battle of Berezovka, which effectively opened the door for the siege of Odessa. The Allies evacuated the city along with any civilians able to obtain a berth from 3 to 6 April and the rape of Odessa ensued.

Meanwhile, the 'Forces Group Crimea' assaulted two seriously depleted White Russian regiments holding the entrances to the Crimean peninsula at Perekop, Chongar and Sivash on 29 March. After several days of fighting, the Reds broke into the Crimea itself on 3 April. Sevastopol, only lightly held by French and Greek forces, came under siege on 15 April. The city fell to the Reds after Allied evacuation on the 28th.

Castigated by critics as a fiasco and largely ignored by historians, Allied intervention in the south arguably achieved one success. The French and Greeks distracted the Reds

The British and Colonel Bicherkov's Cossacks prepare to advance on Baku in the Caucasus. (Imperial War Museum, Q15925)

and gave Romania time to expand its national forces and stabilize defences on the Dniester River. In the meantime, in neighbouring Hungary a communist revolution had taken place under the revolutionary leader, Bela Kun. In response, the Romanians moved decisively against the communists in summer 1919. The fall of Budapest to Romanian troops on 6 August may have prevented the spread of Bolshevism into Central Europe.

The British first intervened in South Russia for another play of what has been called the 'Great Game', namely, protecting the Central Asian approaches to India, their 'jewel in the Crown'. The terms of the Treaty of Brest-Litovsk had ceded three Russian provinces to the Ottoman Empire: Georgia, Armenia and Azerbaijan. These nations had declared independence, however, forming the Trans-Caucasian Commissariat, a defensive league meant to uphold their status as emergent nations. Notwithstanding,

the Ottoman Turks overran Armenia and Azerbaijan in spring 1918. In response, the Georgians invited the Germans to enter in May in order to offset Turkish influence.

Britain, meanwhile, had been seeking to frustrate a takeover of the entire Caucasus region by the Central Powers. British Major-General Lionel Dunsterville was ordered to establish a military mission in the Caucasus and from there rally a new pro-Allied front. Setting out from Baghdad with a small colonial expedition in January 1918, Dunsterville marched northwards through Persia where he allied with a group of Cossacks led by Colonel Bicherakov.

By May, the oil-rich Caspian Sea port of Baku seemed to be the best location for a military mission. Here, a motley collection of Red Guards, Armenians, Azerbaijanis and Russians of every political persuasion had decided to put up resistance to a further Turkish advance. Bicherakov's Cossacks proceeded to Baku in June, Dunsterville's British following in August.

The Turks put Baku under siege from 26 August to 14 September. Determined

Turkish attacks and superior numbers overcame the local contingents and the British themselves were forced to evacuate by sea on the 14th. Fortunes turned, however, when on 30 October 1918, the Ottoman Empire signed an armistice ending Turkish participation in World War One. One of the clauses freed Baku from Ottoman control and allowed the establishment of the British 14th Division in that city.

From there, the British were able to provide assistance to the emergent Caucasian states and to General Denikin's Whites in 1919. In particular, British vessels sporting 4-inch guns were able to fight a Red naval flotilla based at Astrakhan for possession of the Caspian Sea.

Further east, Major-General Wilfred Malleson made another play in the Great Game. The collapse of the Russian Provisional Government and the Bolshevik Revolution had also rocked Central Asia in 1917. New Islamic states and emirates emerged from the broken Russian Empire. These felt threatened by Red propaganda that had entered their cities and by the numbers of newly freed German and Austro-Hungarian prisoners in their midst who seemed to be colluding.

The government of Ashkabad, which had been embroiled in a reign of terror and counter-terror, Red Guards versus Muslims, therefore asked for British assistance in summer 1918. Malleson responded with a battalion of Punjabis based in Persia, moving northeast into the Trans-Caspian region of Turkestan in August. A new anti-Bolshevik force took shape and grew to several thousands, the 'Trans-Caspian Army', which heavily defeated the Reds in October.

Unfortunately, one incident soured relations between the British and the government of Ashkabad that autumn – the execution of the '26 Commissars', an event later made famous in Soviet paintings and propaganda. These Red commissars had escaped from the Turks at Baku and crossed the Caspian to Krasnovodsk on 15 September. Here they were apprehended by local troops and shot. Far from directing the proceedings, the British had protested vehemently.

By January 1919 the British decided that any German-Turkish threat to Central Asia had evaporated; therefore, Malleson was recalled and the last of the British left Trans-Caspia in April. The Trans-Caspian Army, however, fought on until its destruction by the Red Army in summer 1919.

Far to the west, the British intervened in February 1919 at the port of Novorossisk on the Black Sea. Lieutenant-General Briggs originally headed the 500 members of the British Military Mission to South Russia, relinquishing this command to the redoubtable Major-General Sir H. C. Holman that spring. This mission included technicians, logisticians and weapons experts of every kind, sent to train Denikin's Whites in the arts of flying, driving tanks and how to use British artillery and machine guns.

The mission headquartered at Ekaterinodar, 96 kilometres northeast of Novorossisk, in the Kuban. Royal Air Force instructors, having brought 130 RE8 aircraft with them, trained many of the future pilots and observers of Denikin's Air Force at Chernomorskt Aerodrome three kilometres outside Ekaterinodar. Royal Tank Corps instructors were also based in Ekaterinodar from April to June before moving up to the port of Taganrog on the Sea of Azov in summer 1919. Over 200 Whites received driver/gunner training for the mission's 74 tanks (for further information about British–White tank operations see Osprey New Vanguard 83: *Armoured Units of the Russian Civil War: White and Allied*). Many of the Royal Tank Corps personnel seized every opportunity to test their battle skills against the Reds under mobile conditions far different from what they had experienced on the Western Front.

One part of the mission included No. 47 Squadron, Royal Air Force. The squadron, mostly composed of volunteers from Britain and the former Balkan Front, set out from Salonika, Greece, bound for Novorossisk on 16 April 1919. Major (later Air Marshal) Raymond Collishaw commanded. The unit contained several notable personnel including Western Front ace Captain Sam Kinkead, Captain (later

The Bolsheviks believed their world revolution would occur only after industrial Germany, with its large proletariat positioned in the heart of Europe, fell to the Reds. In this photo, members of the Prussian Schutzpolizei pose beside a German Communist Party (KPD) armoured train captured during the Leuna Industrial Complex revolt in Saxony, 23–29 March 1921. The rebels, led by Max Hoelz and numbering 3,000–4,000, had fortified the complex and created this armoured train. Colonel Bernhard Graf von Poninski with 4,000 Schutzpolizei put down the rebellion. Typical of class conflicts everywhere, the event was marred by the torture and execution of prisoners on both sides. (Photo card, Bullock collection)

Air Chief Marshal) William Elliot and Captain Marion Aten, an American volunteer who purportedly attained 'ace' status while in theatre (ranks may appear differently in books because the Royal Air Force changed its rank structure in August 1919).

No. 47 flew DH9, DH9a and Sopwith Camel aircraft and achieved legendary fame while flying from Beketovka Aerodrome, 20 kilometres south of Tsaritsyn, in support of General Baron Wrangel's Caucasian Army. From August to October, No. 47 bombed and strafed two Red naval flotillas threatening the city from the Volga River. 'B' Flight, with the four Sopwith Camels, was especially popular with the Cossacks. In October, the Red Army broke through Wrangel's front, the 5,000-strong cavalry of Dumenko leading the way. Kinkead, Aten and the pilots of 'B' Flight released their bombs on the Red horsemen and followed up with repeated strafing runs. The Cossacks then counter-attacked with their sabres, counting 1,600 enemy bodies at the end of the day.

When ordered to disband in October and become merely instructors, the personnel of

No. 47 volunteered to serve in Denikin's AFSR. Collishaw took a particular interest in attacking Red armoured trains north of the Crimea in February 1920 before the unit handed over its aircraft to the Whites and evacuated on 30 March.

The end of intervention

For the Allies as well as the Russians, the civil war grew out of the final events of World War One. First, the Allies had to reconstitute an Eastern Front against the Central Powers. After the Armistice, the Allies had to frustrate post-war German ambitions, deal with the new nation states that had emerged on the periphery of Russia and prevent the spread of a virulent new revolutionary doctrine, Bolshevism. In practical terms, halting Bolshevism also meant supporting the White Russians.

Most of the Allied troops looked forward to going home and returning to their natural lives. A few embraced the new adventures and became ardent supporters of the Whites. For Western home governments, however, intervention came too soon after World War One to be enticing and the potential threat of communism seemed to distant to be of immediate concern. Most political consitituents wanted to bring the troops home and pressured their governments to do so.

Then again, the events of the civil war moved too quickly. Lacking broad popular support, at each juncture, the cumbersome diplomatic and political engines of the Allies proved unable to catch up to unfolding events, still less to anticipate or control them. Each new challenge brought fresh haggling and positioning as each nation strove to succeed in its own national interests. Unwilling to commit the necessary number of troops to be decisive, the Allies pinned their hopes first on the Czech Legion, next on Kolchak, then Denikin, and finally the newly emergent national states in Eastern Europe. Lack of agreed vision, clarity of purpose and want of sustained determination doomed each enterprise in turn.

Women in the Russian Civil War

For women, distinctions between non-combatant and combatant blurred during the Russian Civil War. The lucky ones lived far behind the lines in areas that were not exposed to the rapidly shifting fronts. Most were housewives, mothers, farm labourers, industrial workers, shopkeepers, telephone operators – in other words, ordinary people concerned with simply staying alive and finding enough food to eat at affordable prices.

Some chose the path of easy virtue, or were forced down that road because of adverse circumstances. According to Bolshevik statistics, the number of women involved in prostitution had gone over the 3 per cent mark in 1917, and, given the increasing privations of the civil war period, this number must have gone still higher. Indeed, first-hand military memoirs, both Red and White, record general acceptance and even appreciation for women who followed the camps cooking, nursing and engaging in occasional prostitution, sometimes the same woman in all three roles. By the early 1920s, after the wreck of the White Armies in the Far East and the general collapse of the economy, Oriental 'gentlemen' with the money to partake used the words 'prostitute' or '*kurvy*' and 'Russian girl' interchangeably.

The Bolshevik Revolution afforded some women the luxury of promoting their particular version of feminism, such as the progressive visions espoused by the Bolshevik

The civil war in Russian Palekh art style glorifying the role of the new Soviet woman: female, nurse (see medical bag), and soldier. (Painting by A. Kurkin, Sovietsky Kudoshnik art card)

theorist Alexandra Kollontai. Kollontai, who had been at Smolny with Lenin during the October Revolution, held various positions promoting the rights of women, including the post of Commissar of Public Welfare. Kollontai's views, however, were well ahead of their time and based on an agenda more suitable to rapidly developing Western nations. Although increasingly marginalized politically, she served the Bolsheviks loyally through to the 1940s.

Rather than promoting a separate movement for women or viewing feminism as an exercise in individual rights, Lenin's own wife, Nadezhda Krupskaya, promoted the cause of women within the Party itself. Women were, in a sense, 'nationalized' and yoked with the men, equal in theory, as part of a team plodding along the path towards a new socialist dawn. To this end, women featured prominently in period posters and paintings in the roles of farm labourers, industrial workers, political activists, teachers, nurses and even soldiers, alongside their male counterparts.

Many foreign women were swept up in the events inside Russia, either by circumstance or by choice. British subject Doreen Stanford lived in Siberia from 1916 to 1920 while her father worked as a mining engineer south of Krasnoyarsk in an area frequented by the Red partisan leader Shchetinkin. Her memoirs portray the hardships experienced by the people in the rural areas touched by civil war. Katia Swan, with her husband Alfred, both members of the American Red Cross, spent 1918–21 working among needy and orphaned children who had been evacuated to the Urals and Western Siberia. Swedish nurse Elsa Brandstrom coordinated international relief agencies caring for and helping to repatriate the hundreds of thousands of prisoners of war left in Russia and Siberia after the end of World War One. These are notable examples, but only a few among many.

For female civilians, travelling in the heat of civil war could be a precarious undertaking, but it was sometimes safer than remaining in place. Baroness Sophie Buxhoeveden, a lady-in-waiting to the Empress Alexandra, had been with the tsar's family at Tsarkoe Selo where they had been confined after the February Revolution in 1917. When Nicholas and Alexandra and their children were transferred to the Kornilov House in Tobolsk, Siberia, in August, Sophie had remained behind for a surgical operation. Upon recovery, she determined to rejoin them, receiving her travelling papers in Petrograd from the Kerensky government on 6 November, one day before the Bolshevik Revolution. Only overcrowding on the train prevented the commissars of the new regime from discovering her identity.

She remained in contact with the royal family in Tobolsk only through letters that were highly censored by the local authorities, her own movements being under constant observation. Then, after the Bolsheviks had established their control more securely in April 1918, Nicholas, Alexandra and Marie were transferred to the Ipatiev House in Ekaterinburg. Sophie escorted the second party, consisting of Olga, Tatiana, Anastasia, Alexei and the household staff to Ekaterinburg in May.

By mid-July, the Whites and the Czech Legion were approaching the city and the Bolsheviks decided to liquidate the royal family to prevent their capture. Sophie was not present on the fateful night of 17 July when a Chekist squad under the command of Yakov Yurovsky shot Nicholas and Alexandra multiple times in the chest and head, nor did she hear the dull thuds of the rifle butts or the silent, probing work of the bayonets that dispatched their children. A week after her arrival, the Bolsheviks had ordered her and several members of the staff to return to Tobolsk.

After experiencing two weeks of chaos on the railways, her journey ended at Tiumen because Tobolsk had fallen to the Whites. The green and white flag of the Provisional Government of Siberia replaced the red flag at Tiumen in mid- July. Sophie rode in a Czech Legion train to Omsk in January 1919, travelling to Vladivostok the following month on board a former imperial court

'The White Angel', Varvara N., female soldier,
1st Battalion, Kornilov Shock Regiment.
(Photo, Hutchinson & Co, 1938)

road that ran parallel to the railway bed, and was only wide enough for two sleds to pass side by side. The even less fortunate walked.

The legend of women warriors had always existed in Russia, but not until 1917 were thousands brought together as soldiers. Had Russia not descended into revolution and civil war later that autumn, these would have seen active service on the Eastern Front in 1918. A peasant woman who already had been on active duty since 1915, Maria 'Yashka' Leontevna Botchkareva organized the First Russian Women's Battalion of Death in Petrograd in May 1917. This unit fought valiantly at the front in July and was heavily bloodied.

As female volunteers stepped forward by the thousand, two more units, the First Petrograd Women's Battalion and the Second Moscow Women's Battalion of Death followed in June. The 1st Petrograd Women's Battalion received much attention from international journalists and was visited by the noted British feminist Emmeline Pankhurst. The 3rd Kuban Women's Shock Battalion and the 1st Women's Naval Detachment activated in July.

Valentina Petrova, herself a Russian St George Cross winner for valour, just like Botchkareva, even approached Kerensky for permission to organize the women's Black Hussars of Death. One unit under formation in Baku sported the skull and crossbones on its flag with the motto, 'For the freedom of Russia – the Women's Battalion of Death'. Other units operated informally and even attached themselves to men's shock regiments that were already at the front.

Uncomfortable with what they viewed as bourgeois women with guns, the Bolsheviks labelled the women's units 'counter-revolutionary' and ordered their disbandment in November 1917. Some of these units retained their cohesion into the early months of 1918, an undetermined number of individuals undoubtedly dispersing into the new White, nationalist and even Red armies engaging in civil war.

Women, in fact, served in every army on every front in every phase of the Russian Civil

train with Major-General Sir Alfred Knox, head of the British Military Mission in Siberia, and thereafter into exile.

Other women experienced even more dangerous conditions on the railways. Olga Ilyin, whose brother was chief engineer of the illustrious Izhevsk-Votkinsk Division, retreated with the Czechs and Whites from Kazan in autumn 1918 and spent 1919 in Omsk as a translator of American, French and English newspapers. Her second brother was in the White infantry while a third was a primary organizer of the Kazan Dragoons.

Before she successfully escaped to America, Olga became embroiled in the White retreat through the winter of 1919–20, a nightmare odyssey of hunger, disease, exposure, frostbite, partisan attacks and death. Those who could not find a place in the trains that were overflowing with desperate refugees rode sleds along the Great Siberian Highway, or Sibirsky Trakt. The Trakt was a frozen dirt

War. Their roles varied from administrative work to logistical support, to direct battlefield participation as combatants and nurses. Judging from contemporary memoirs, nearly all expected to be raped or worse if captured by an opposing force. In not a few instances, these fears were fully realized.

The young Kuban Cossack Marina Yurlova was one example of a woman soldier who served in World War One then continued fighting in the Russian Civil War. Marina joined the Reconnaissance Sotnia (100 horse squadron) of the 3rd Ekaterinodar Regiment in 1914 at the age of 14. Over the next three years she was shot in the leg while blowing a bridge and received concussion from an exploding shell on the Caucasus Front. Then in Persia in 1917, while driving for the Red Cross, she received another more serious concussion resulting in shell-shock. In all, she received three St George Crosses for bravery.

After receiving treatment over the next year in various hospitals, including finally at Kazan, Marina was mobilized into Colonel V. O. Kappel's White forces fighting alongside the Czech Legion for possession of the city. Briefly assigned to defending the arsenal and ammunition factory, she was later shot in the shoulder by Red Guards while on reconnaissance. During the retreat from Kazan on 10/11 September she was evacuated by medical cart while under bombardment by Bolshevik aircraft. After recovery in a hospital in Omsk, Marina crossed the Trans-Siberian with the help of a Czech officer and emigrated from Vladivostok in April 1919.

Yashka Botchkareva, eager to continue the fight against the Central Powers, travelled to Archangel after the Allies landed in August 1918 and offered to raise a new women's Battalion of Death. Embarrassed, and not as able to envisage female combat soldiers as the Russians of 1917 had been, British General Sir Edmund Ironside sidestepped her plans. Still determined, Yashka travelled to Siberia in April 1919 and formed a women's medical detachment under Admiral Kolchak. After the defeat of the Whites, she returned to her

Wounded cossack Woman from Ural Front

Женщина казак ранена на Уральском фронтѣ.

This photo's original caption is correct, but fails to credit the subject as Marina Yurlova. A duplicate photo exists, without the caption, in her memoirs *Cossack Girl*. (Allied photo card, 1919, Bullock collection).

home in Tomsk where the Cheka captured her. After four months of rigorous interrogation, she was executed on 16 May 1920.

One of the most remarkable women of the civil war period was a striking and charismatic Don Cossack, the granddaughter of Baron Fredericks, Varvara 'Varia' N., nicknamed 'The White Angel of the White Army' by her companions. After experiencing the horrors of the Bolshevik occupation of Taganrog in late autumn 1917, Varvara escaped to Novocherkassk to join the Volunteer Army in December at the age of 21. She enlisted under her own name in the Kornilov Shock Regiment (five other women of noble background joined under false names).

She was wounded three times in 1918 (shrapnel in the jaw, internal bleeding from the percussion of an exploding shell, and a knife wound to the left leg) and additionally survived the deadly Spanish influenza. In 1919 she took a dum-dum bullet to the left leg and

was hit again in the left knee while aboard a White armoured train north of Kharkov. Varvara killed at least two men – a Red Circassian in 1918 at close range, as well as

Pavlina Ivanovna Kuznetsova served as a machine-gunner on a *tachanka* in the 6th Chongarsky Division, 1st Horse Army. (Painting by L. Kotliarov, Sovietsky Kudoshnik art card).

executing one spy in 1919. A crack shot, she probably accounted for many more at longer range.

Still suffering from her wounds, ill with fever and weakened from the privations of a long retreat, she evacuated Russia from the port of Novorossisk for England on 6 April 1920 with the help of the gallant and pro-White head of the British Military Mission, General Holman. Varvara withheld her last name from her autobiography, using the pseudonym 'Lul Gardo' for her 1930s publication, in order to protect those close to her still inside Russia. Even so, her only child, Eugenie, died of starvation in a Soviet prison.

The Reds also had their women soldiers, many thousands in the support services and many hundreds who took up arms. One splendid example was the 22-year-old beauty Larissa Reissner, who, according to literary critics, served as the physical prototype for 'Lara' in Boris Pasternak's monumental epic *Doctor Zhivago*. In 1918, Reissner married Fedor Raskolnikov, commander of the Volga Flotilla, and served as the fleet's political officer in charge of intelligence during combat operations along the Volga and Kama Rivers from July through to November.

Larissa participated in the Red counter-attack on Kazan in September 1918. During those autumn days she worked closely with Trotsky and recalled in her 1920s book *Front* his inspirational 'holy demagoguery of battle'. Her feelings were reciprocated, Trotsky describing her in his memoirs as an 'Olympian goddess who combined a subtle, ironical wit with the courage of a warrior'.

During the winter of 1918–19, Reissner acted as naval commissar in Moscow before returning to operational duty aboard the Astrakhan-Caspian and Volga-Caspian Flotillas from June 1919 to June 1920. Here she pioneered the concept of mounted naval reconnaissance, taking part in the fighting against the Whites at Tsaritsyn and Astrakhan and against the British at Enzeli in Azerbaijan. She died of typhus in 1926 at the age of 30, after inspiring Pasternak's poem 'Lara' that same year.

The equally youthful Dr Raisa Azarkh

served alternately as medical chief and political commissar on the Volga, Ukrainian and Far Eastern Fronts from 1918 to 1920. During these years, she astutely organized field and hospital facilities in Viatka, Kiev, Omsk and Krasnoyarsk. As commissar of the Viatka Special Division, she fought against the Whites in the Kama Valley in autumn 1918, then transferred to the Ukraine from December 1918 to July 1919.

While in the Ukraine, Dr Azarkh established her mobile headquarters inside a railcar, medical wagon no. 202, which was occasionally attached to armoured trains for protection. She saw action against the troops of Petlyura, Grigoriev and Denikin while aboard armoured trains, finishing her civil war experience in Siberia and the Far East from autumn 1919 to autumn 1920.

Rozalia Samoylova-Zemliachka served as political commissar on the Southern Front in 1918–20. She spent November 1918 to September 1919 attached to the 8th Army fighting against the Don Cossacks. From 8 October 1919, at the time of the greatest danger to Moscow from Denikin's Whites, she fought in the beleaguered 13th Army. Her forte was political indoctrination, training and teamwork. Among her comrades she was known as a strict disciplinarian. Her enemies knew her as a middle-aged Jewess who dressed in black leathers and killed with passion.

Zemliachka demonstrated her revolutionary fervour after the evacuation of Wrangel's Whites in November 1920. Here, she played a prominent role in the massacre of 50,000 men, women and children in the Crimea along with her compatriot, the Hungarian communist executioner Bela Kun. For this 'political work' she received the Order of the Red Banner in 1921.

Alexandra 'Shura' Permyakova participated in the capture of Moscow during the October Revolution in 1917. After obtaining critical intelligence about White Guard strengths and positions, she joined the Red Guards in the assault on the Kremlin. In 1918 she stayed in Moscow, engaging in political work, writing a training course for commissars and combating black marketeers and counter-revolutionaries.

Shura spent 1919 on the Southern Front as chief of the political section of the 15th Inzenskaya Division, the division in which her husband was commissar. She remained on the Southern Front throughout 1920, taking part in the desperate hand-to-hand fighting at Kakhovka in October, where her husband was bayoneted.

The following month, Shura met Red commander Mikhail Frunze personally and volunteered to be in the advance group crossing the dangerous Sivash marshes at night, an adventure that outflanked the nearly impregnable White positions in the Crimea. Only 70 of the original 270 volunteers survived the treacherous bogs and gunfire. She won the Order of the Red Banner for conspicuous gallantry.

One Bolshevik female left a legacy of horror. The Whites discovered a ghastly charnel house of torture, mutilation and dismemberment after their occupation of Kiev in 1919. This dungeon had served as the unholy playground of the notorious Cheka agent known locally as 'Rosa'. British General J. F. C. Fuller, who had been sent out to inspect the White Tank Corps, travelled to Kiev and published an 'anonymous' article independently confirming these events for the international community.

Other women originally assisted the Bolsheviks but turned against them in the face of increasing state centralism or for patriotic reasons after the punitive Treaty of Brest-Litovsk. One example was Maria Spiridonova, a prominent leader of the Left Socialist Revolutionaries who had assassinated a tsarist general in her youth. Disenchanted with Bolshevik policies, Maria was a major force organizing her party's revolt in July 1918. Konstantin Paustovsky, attending an assembly of journalists at the Bolshoi Theatre in Moscow, witnessed her dramatic announcement of the 'revolution' seconds before Red Guards began engaging the insurgents in the streets: 'Heels clicking, a woman in black, a scarlet carnation pinned to her blouse, ran across the stage towards the footlights … the woman held a small steel pistol. She raised her arm, pointed it at the ceiling and, with another clatter of heels, cried piercingly: "Hurrah for the rebellion!".' After the abortive coup, Spiridonova passed her remaining years in hiding, in exile or in prison until her final execution by Soviet security forces in 1941.

Another Socialist Revolutionary, Fanya Kaplan, had embraced the October Revolution but turned against the Bolsheviks for the same reasons as Spiridonova. By summer 1918 she had established connections with British master spy Sidney Reilly, connections that remain mysterious to the present day. On 30 August she attempted to assassinate Lenin in Moscow, succeeding in shooting him in his suit coat, his shoulder and jaw. After a brisk interrogation in which she refused to betray her associates, she was executed on 3 September.

Women were also prominent in the Anarchist movement. Although few served in the front lines, several thousand supported Makhno's logistical system, provided intelligence and medical services, and acted as couriers between the outlying partisan bands. A local observer, M. Gutman, recalled seeing a group of Anarchist females dressed entirely in black entering Ekaterinoslav with Makhno's main forces in 1919. The hue of these uniforms served a double purpose, black being the colour of the Anarchist movement as well as indicating a certain elite status or dedication.

Makhno's own constant companion, the tall, beautiful and dignified Galina Kuzmenko, a former teacher from Gulyai-Polye, served in his intelligence department and by reputation was equally adroit with the rifle and machine gun. One of the most colourful was Maroussia Nikiforova, who raised a Black Guard partisan unit of several hundred in Alexandrovsk in the last half of 1917. Dressed in black leathers and riding a white horse, she terrorized landlords and institutions until her execution at the hands of General Slaschev's Whites at Simferopol in autumn 1919.

1920–22

Destruction of the AFSR

The AFSR retreated in the late autumn and early winter of 1919 in good order, pressed all along the line from Poland to the Volga. Red numerical superiority ensured that the Whites almost always had one or more of their flanks turned in a given sector. In particular, Red cavalry maintained pressure on the junction between the Volunteer and Don Armies. In this area also lay the primary rail lines through which the Whites had to retreat. Severance of any part of the railway meant units were trapped and ultimately destroyed.

Failing to hold Kursk, the AFSR attempted to defend Kharkov to the south. A bottleneck of trains, filled with retreating troops and civilians sympathetic to the White cause, began at Kharkov and continued all the way

to Rostov. Outflanked to the west, Kharkov fell on 11 December. Typhus set in with what would become a particularly harsh winter. By January 1920, over 42,000 White soldiers lay wounded or stricken with the epidemic.

White commanders in the west, pressed by the 12th and 14th Armies, also retreated. Kiev fell on 16 December. Shilling's forces retired towards Odessa and the Crimea. The 5th Cavalry Corps, reorganized as the 1st Cavalry Division because of combat losses, was down to the strength of a small regiment by 17 December. Bredov's troops, cut off, tried to fall back on Romania, but being turned away by gunfire, retreated northwest to be interned by Poland. Slaschev's Corps cut its way through Makhno's partisans in time to secure the entrances to the Crimea, behind which survivors could rally. On 7 February, Odessa endured its third tragic evacuation.

In the east, Tsaritsyn fell on 3 January, prompting a withdrawal of the Caucasian Army and North Caucasian Detachment to the southwest, back, essentially, to the starting lines of early 1919. In the general confusion, Denikin relocated his headquarters from Taganrog, to Rostov, to Tikhoretskaya, to Ekaterinodar and finally to Novorossisk. These relocations reflected the fate of the AFSR. From 5 to 8 January, Red cavalry took Taganrog, Novocherkassk and Rostov.

Cossack morale had collapsed between November 1919 and March 1920. Once more the Don *voisko* fell under occupation. Troops deserted wholesale to protect their families. Cossack nationalists in the Kuban agitated for independence and, threatening to

Semyon Mikhailovich Budenny, commander of the 1st Horse Army, 1919–20, by L. Kotliarov. He became a Marshal of the Soviet Union in 1935. (Soviet art card, c. 1930)

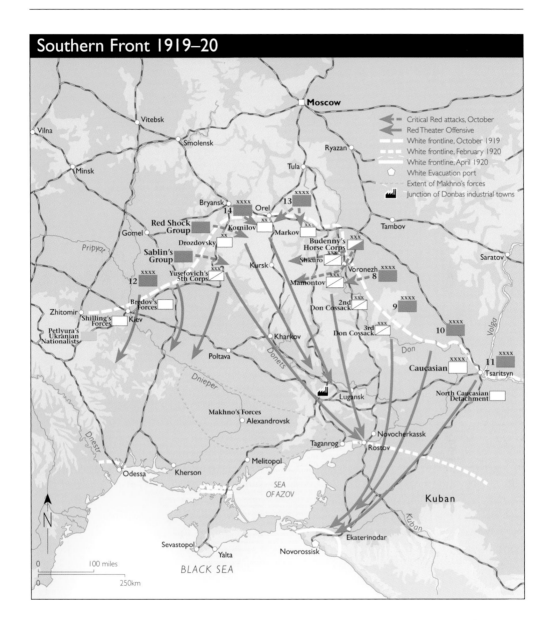

Southern Front 1919–20

Legend:
- Critical Red attacks, October
- Red Theater Offensive
- White frontline, October 1919
- White frontline, February 1920
- White frontline, April 1920
- White Evacuation port
- Extent of Makhno's forces
- Junction of Donbas industrial towns

Map labels: Moscow, Vitebsk, Vilna, Smolensk, Ryazan, Tula, Minsk, Bryansk, Orel, 13, 14, Red Shock Group, Kornilov, Markov, Tambov, Gomel, Drozdovsky, Budenny's Horse Corps, Pripyat, Sablin's Group, Kursk, Shkuro, Saratov, 12, Yusefovich's 5th Corps, Voronezh, 8, Mamontov, Bredov's Forces, Zhitomir, Shilling's Forces, Kiev, 2nd Don Cossack, 9, Petlyura's Ukranian Nationalists, Kharkov, 3rd Don Cossack, 10, Don, Volga, Poltava, Caucasian, 11, Tsaritsyn, Dnieper, Donets, North Caucasian Detachment, Lugansk, Makhno's Forces, Alexandrovsk, Dniestr, Taganrog, Novocherkassk, Rostov, Melitopol, Kuban, Odessa, Kherson, SEA OF AZOV, N, Sevastopol, Yalta, Novorossisk, Ekaterinodar, Kuban, BLACK SEA, 0 100 miles, 0 250km

overturn their government, had to be quelled in a show of force by General Pokrovsky in November.

The AFSR partially rallied in January–February, scoring several successes on the Don River and at Rostov and Bataisk. However, the Red 1st Cavalry Army outflanked the line in the east. A corps of White cavalry, consisting of Don, Kuban, Terek and Astrakhan Cossacks and the remnants of the Russian Guard Cavalry, attempted to halt the breakthrough in mid-February. After a forced march in sub-zero temperatures, the Whites literally bumped into the Reds, surprising both sides. Thousands drew sabres and interpenetrated each other's ranks in *mêlée*. One White veteran of this battle confided to the author that his Guards cavalry had not thought themselves defeated, for the Red regiment opposing theirs eventually retired. Nevertheless, in subsequent encounters the Reds flanked the line.

The renewed Kuban line also failed to hold, Ekaterinodar falling on 17 March. The Whites were now pushed back onto the port

(Left) Ataman Vdovenko of the Terek Cossacks, (centre left) Ataman Bogaevsky of the Don Cossacks, (centre right) Ataman Filimonov of the Kuban Cossacks, (right) Ataman Liakov of the Astrakhan Cossacks. (Photo, Ocherki Russkoi Smuty, 1921–1925)

of Novorossisk from which they hoped to evacuate by ship to the Crimea. While Denikin requested Allied naval assistance and prepared the White Navy for evacuation, the Volunteer 1st Corps held the mountains north of the city. Rebels calling themselves 'Greens' took control of the Black Sea coast and attacked White trains, stragglers and isolated units.

The early stages of the evacuation went smoothly enough, units that still had cohesion embarking first. Allied munitions, including tanks and aircraft, were dumped into the bay. On 27 March, units of the 1st Corps withdrew from the forward positions and prepared to embark. Reds and Greens entered the suburbs of Novorossisk in their wake, sporadic firing breaking out in the streets. Now positioned on the hills above, the Reds commenced shelling the doomed city.

As the too-few ships began to sail away, chaos ensued. Crowds surged towards the docks and the safety of the ships that for so many meant life or death. Profiteers made fortunes from any boat or berth that could still be bought as families and comrades were torn apart. Cossacks embraced then shot their horses at the docks, scores then shooting themselves.

In the harbour, the French ship *Waldeck Rousseau* and the British ship *Empress of India* opened counter-battery fire on the Red artillery. Denikin, remaining to the last, witnessed the fires raging and the pall of smoke. Suddenly, a White destroyer, the *Pylki*, dashed back in and with guns blazing rescued a regiment of the Drozdovsky that had been the final rearguard. As his ship pulled away Denikin reflected: 'After this, everything grew quiet. The contours of the city, the shoreline, and mountains became misty as they receded into the distance … into the past … the hard and painful past.'

Last stand of the Whites

General Baron Petr Wrangel assumed command of the shattered AFSR upon Denikin's resignation on 4 April 1920. Immediately, Wrangel renamed his Whites 'The Russian Army' on 11 May and forbade the use of the tricolor chevron on uniforms in order to build a new force, a new morale. The classes of 1900 and 1901 were mobilized on the 15th. Ships sailed to rendezvous with and collect pockets of troops left behind along the Black Sea coastline. A new government and a new army had to be created quickly.

The Russian Army's diplomatic situation was desperate. Britain offered little if any help and made it clear that if the Whites moved beyond the Crimea diplomatic relations would cease. Britain, under the leadership of David Lloyd George, had already written off the Whites and looked instead towards better relations with the Bolsheviks. France talked eloquently about aid and good relations, but made tough economic bargains and sent little. France's diplomatic policy rested on creating alliances with the new nation states in Eastern Europe – Poland, Czechoslovakia and Romania – as a *cordon sanitaire* against the infection of Bolshevism on the one hand, and as a hedge against German imperialism on the other. French support would be conditional on Wrangel's ability to be useful to that scheme.

Wrangel, therefore, determined to be pragmatic. In his own words: 'With the devil and for Russia, but against the Bolsheviks.' Consequently, he sought alliances with Poland, Georgia, Petlyura and Makhno. Poland dispatched a military mission to the Crimea in response while Makhno hanged the White emissaries on the spot.

The Polish were wary of *any* Russians, however, and began their own advance into the Ukraine on 24 April against the Red Army in order to recreate the 'Greater Poland' they had enjoyed during the Middle Ages. This 'Russo-Polish War' would last until 12 October. Although not aimed at helping the fortunes of the Russian Army, the Polish offensive nevertheless distracted the growing might of the Reds and bought Wrangel time to organize.

Strategically, he was in a good position. The Crimea was a peninsula with only two entrances: one natural, one man-made. The first was the Perekop peninsula, a land bridge

General Baron Pyotr Nikolaevich Wrangel had commanded cavalry in the Russo-Japanese War and World War One. His rise in the White Army was meteoric – commanding a cavalry division in August 1918, the Caucasian Army from spring 1919, the Volunteer Army from December 1919, finally becoming commander-in-chief of the new Russian Army on 4 April 1920. Brilliant and charismatic, his tall, imperious figure, dressed in a Cossack *cherkesska*, allowed the Bolsheviks to caricature him as Russia's 'Black Baron'. (Photo, Beloe Delo, 1924)

connecting the Crimea to the mainland, nowhere wider than eight kilometres. From east to west lay the Turkish Wall, a rampart with a deep ditch that the Crimean Khans had once dredged so that the sea could fill as a moat against marauding Zaporozhian Cossacks. The second was the Taganach Bridge connecting the town of that name with the Chongar peninsula on the mainland. There were, of course, the salt marshes of the Sivash, northeast of Perekop, consisting of tide pools so deep that one could only cross by boat. High winds were known to have blown and dried these pools for a period of a few hours, but only a few times each century.

Wrangel formed his 'Government of South Russia', with A. Krivoshein and

Flight of the Bourgeoisie at Novorossisk, 1920 by I. Vladimirov. (Soviet art card, 1930)

P. Struve heading, respectively, domestic and foreign affairs. Wrangel himself took the title 'ruler' in the same vein as had the other White leaders, ultimately concentrating civil and military power into the hands of one man. This arrangement would end when the Russian people finally were able to elect their own representatives in a properly constituted constituent assembly. The new government further promulgated a liberal law that recognized previous peasant seizures of estates while offering compensation for the landowners, a law meant to secure the support of the peasantry. In keeping with her Eastern diplomatic policy, France recognized the new government *de facto* in June 1920.

Geographically, the Government of South Russia controlled the Crimea, a zone of about 25,000 square kilometres known administratively as the South Tauride (or Taurida). They did not control the North Tauride, an area of about 39,000 square miles that followed the Dnieper River from the Black Sea to Alexandrovsk, then southeast towards Berdiansk on the Sea of Azov.

The fertile black soil of the North Tauride grew oats, barley, wheat, rye, potatoes and tobacco, not to mention fruits, farm animals and horses. These products could be traded to international customers in exchange for materials the Whites lacked. Equally important, in addition to the indigenous population, the new government had to feed a quarter of a million mouths that included their army and administration as well as the mass of White sympathizers and refugees who had fled the Red Terror.

Wrangel determined, therefore, to advance into the North Tauride in June, even though such an advance would cost the support of Great Britain. By early June, the army consisted of 25,000 former Volunteers and 10,000 Cossacks. These were divided into three formations: the 1st Corps under Kutepov at the Perekop defences, the Crimean Corps under Slaschev at the Chongar positions and the Don Corps in reserve at Dzhankoi. Opposing these were 20,000 combat effectives of the Red 13th Army.

At 2 am on 7 June White tanks of the 1st Corps began moving towards the first line of Red defences on the Perekop peninsula, snagging the barbed-wire entanglements, turning and ripping them outward. The Kornilov Shock Division charged through the gaps. Overhead, artillery from both sides shattered the quiet night while the heavy guns from the White Navy thundered into the Red positions. Then, before dawn, green bursts from exploding flares signalled that the first line had been taken. The 1st Corps surged forward onto the second line. The Whites secured the peninsula on the 9th and by 13 June the Red 13th Army had been pushed beyond the Dnieper River, hotly pursued by General Babiev's Kuban Cavalry Division.

The right flank also moved on 7 June. General Pisarev's tanks and infantry crashed into the Red positions at Salkovo, while General Slaschev, landing by sea, outflanked the Reds to the east and advanced on Melitopol, taking the city on 10 June. By the 17th, much of the Northern Tauride district was in White hands. The Red 13th Army had lost 8,000 men and much *matériel*.

The Reds counter-attacked at the end of June. Dmitry Zhloba's 1st Horse Corps with attached infantry regiments, a force numbering 13,500, moved southwest towards Melitopol, while the 13th Army pressured the Dnieper River line. Two assaults on the Dnieper were hurled back. Zhloba himself had to make night marches because by day White aircraft pinpointed then strafed his troops. Outnumbered, the Don Corps facing Zhloba retired.

Wrangel, however, had planned a Cannae for 2–3 July. While the elite divisions of the 1st Corps moved east against the Red right and centre, the Cossacks wheeled to the Red left and rear. Several units of infantry lay in wait in a series of villages across Zhloba's path. Other infantry units, equipped with armoured cars and *tachanki* machine-gun carts, moved forward to engage the Red cavalry on open ground. Elements of the White 2nd Corps equipped with armoured cars closed the gap in the enemy rear. Hit on all sides, and strafed by White aircraft, the Reds panicked, and, desperately seeking a way out, ran into a series of ambushes. Only a few hundred survived.

Trooper of the Empress Marie Feodorovna's Cuirassiers Regiment, the 'Blue Curisassiers'. This unit was brigaded with other former imperial Guard Cavalry regiments such as the 'Yellow Cuirassiers' and the 'Horse Guards' to form the (White) Guard Cavalry Division in Yusefovich's 5th Cavalry Corps in 1919 and Wrangel's 1st Cavalry Division in 1920. (Russian art card, c. 1910s).

Despite the war with Poland, Red reinforcements continued to arrive throughout July from northern and eastern Russia. On 7 August the Reds crossed the Dnieper using boats and established a bridgehead at Kakhovka. Pontoon bridges were constructed. White attempts to reduce the bridgehead had all but failed by 13 August. Simultaneously, in the east the Red 2nd Horse Army with four infantry divisions maintained steady pressure on the White 1st Corps. Losses on both sides were heavy.

Understanding that he was facing a war of attrition, Wrangel tried to raise more troops by sending an expedition into the Kuban under General Ulagai in August. This force, consisting of 5,000 cavalry and infantry, 130 machine guns, eight aircraft, a detachment of armoured cars and 26 pieces of artillery, landed on the 14th and headed inland towards Ekaterinodar. The Bolsheviks, however, had already learned of the landing and a general uprising by the Cossacks against them did not occur. On 23 August, Ulagai decided to retreat back to the coast. Despite overall failure and sharp rearguard actions, the Kuban expedition safely re-embarked on 1 September with an additional 5,000 Cossacks on board.

Wrangel now received news from his agents in Warsaw that the Poles were considering an armistice with the Reds. This event would release additional enemy armies onto his fronts along the Dnieper and the Northern and Eastern Tauride. In anticipation of this, Kutepov's 1st Army held the left flank, the Dnieper River line, from the sea to Alexandrovsk, including positions extending to the right of the city. Here stood the elite 1st Corps and the Kuban Cavalry. General Abramov commanded the 2nd Army on the right flank with the Don Corps and former units of the Crimean Corps. Considering the coming armistice, the Poles released General Bredov and 8,000 White troops who had been operating in the Russo-Polish War and these arrived by ship in the Crimea.

Wrangel determined not to wait for the attritional onslaught, but to manoeuvre and disrupt Red positions before their reinforcements arrived. After unsuccessful attempts to reduce the Kakhovka bridgehead throughout August–October, the Whites organized the 'Trans-Dnieper Operation'.

This operation took place between 6 and 16 October. While the 1st Corps threw its armoured units and infantry against the trenches and barbed-wire positions at Kakhovka, other infantry, including Kuban cavalry, crossed north of the Kakhovka bridgehead at Uchelka and constructed a pontoon. For three days they captured and held Nikopol. Meanwhile, the Markov Division anchored the northernmost White defences at Khortitsa Island in Alexandrovsk. The Kornilov Shock Division with Kuban cavalry crossed the Dnieper at Khortitsa and moved southwest.

If successful, the entire Red front on the Dnieper would have been dislocated and White units could have continued southwest, encircling and destroying the Kakhovka bridgehead. Unfortunately, the centre column did not move decisively and the Kuban cavalry lost their hero, Babiev, who received his 20th and final wound. This group and the Kornilov column both encountered unexpected Red reinforcements and decided to withdraw on 13 October. In fact, the anticipated armistice between Poland and the Bolsheviks had taken place the day before.

By mid-October, the Reds were free to transfer the majority of their combat troops against the southern Whites. On the White left stood the Red 6th Army and the 1st Horse Army; in the centre, the 2nd Horse and 4th Armies; and on the right, the 13th Army. Having temporarily made an armistice with the Reds, Nestor Makhno additionally contributed a brigade from his insurgent army, the majority mounted on horses or *tachanki*. In all, there were 188,000 infantry, cavalry and engineers with 3,000 machine guns, 600 artillery pieces and 23 armoured trains, not including Makhno's special *tachanki* machine-gun regiment.

Opposing this array were the White 1st and 2nd Armies consisting of 23,000 infantry and 12,000 cavalry. Each army contained component infantry and cavalry units and aviation, armoured car, armoured train and tank detachments. When the general front-wide offensive commenced on 25 October, Wrangel was in little doubt about his enemy's strategy. Combined with continuous pressure all along his lines, the 1st Horse Army intended to cut a swathe to Salkovo and trap the majority of his armies in the North Tauride, preventing their retirement into the Crimea.

Outnumbered five to one, the Whites fought valiantly in the Tauride. Some units lost cohesion and were overrun by the two horse armies. Once again, the 1st Corps lost half its men in savage rearguard actions. Despite desperate hours at the Salkovo pass, Kutepov and Abramov succeeded in

Waiting for the enemy. (Russian painting, 1910s)

extricating their forces, entering the more defensible Crimea on 2 November.

Both sides now girded for the critical defence of the Crimea. Wrangel placed all White defences under the command of his most reliable, most steady of generals, Kutepov. Unable to be strong everywhere, the Whites heavily defended Perekop and left a strong garrison at the Taganach Bridge. Smaller garrisons were placed at Kerch and along the Sivash.

Miraculously, on the night of the third anniversary of the Revolution, 7/8 November, high, howling winds came and blew the Sivash dry for several hours. Local civilians loyal to the Reds informed them of this unusual phenomenon. If the Bolsheviks had believed in God, they would have assumed that Moses had returned to part the 'Red' Sea on their behalf. As it was, their god was the Revolution and the opportunity seemed clear enough. Two divisions of Red troops moved rapidly through the shallow and now less treacherous marshes.

Surprised, General Fostikov and his Kuban Cossack garrison opened fire. Rushing forward in the darkness, torpedoes affixed on long poles to explode holes in the strands of barbed wire, the Reds seized then developed a bridgehead. Ominously, the winds slackened just before dawn and the tidal basin began to fill again, trapping the advance force from their comrades on the mainland. Though their position was potentially desperate, they

The assault on the Turkish Wall, Perekop, November 1920. The ditch in front is approximately 8 metres deep. The rampart at the top was reinforced by earth, wood and in several places by concrete and steel plates. The Whites had heavy naval guns in key positions, field artillery and machine-gun nests. Due to the dearth of barbed wire, only a few strands were available at the top. (Bullock photo from Central Armed Forces Museum, Moscow)

had flanked the almost impregnable Turkish Wall from the southeast.

The Reds now threw their full weight against the key to the White positions, the Turkish Wall on Perekop, opening a devastating artillery barrage. Refusing to be silenced, the Whites replied. That day, the Whites threw back three massive attacks by Red infantry, which came on so thickly that soldiers in several of the regiments were packed shoulder to shoulder. Red casualties mounted in the thousands under the withering fire of White artillery canister and machine guns.

The fourth assault came in darkness in the early morning hours of 9 November. As the Whites fired flares to illuminate the charging enemy, both sides traded grenades up and down the ditch below the ramparts. Finally, Red assault troops climbed up and surged over the Turkish Wall.

In response, the Whites were forced back

to their secondary positions, a series of light trenches and machine-gun nests between the lakes of Yushin. This retreat allowed the Reds at Perekop and the Sivash to unite. The Whites held Yushin for two desperate days of attack and counter-attack. Yet again, the 1st Corps lost over half its strength. On 11 November, Kutepov, assessing his threadbare units against the seemingly inexhaustible Red reserves, told Wrangel the end had come.

That day, Wrangel ordered his troops to disengage and fall back to assigned ports for evacuation from the Crimea. Schedules had already been worked out for soldiers and civilians, and ships had been assigned to each of the Crimean ports at Eupatoria, Sevastopol, Yalta, Theodosia and Kerch. Everything that could float had been commandeered: 126 ships in all between the assets of the White and French navies.

The orderly embarkation took three days from the 14th to the 16th. In the end, 145,693 Whites sailed to Constantinople and into exile, to be scattered by the four winds to every distant corner of the world. Following just hours behind, the Red Army settled into the Crimea and 'political' units set to work. In the next weeks some 50,000 'politically unreliable' elements were rounded up and shot.

The end in the Far East

After much deliberation, the Whites decided not to defend their capital at Omsk in November 1919. A sharp downturn in the weather froze the River Irtysh solid, negating its natural defensive value. Instead, a new capital would be established at Irkutsk where the army could rest and replenish. Admiral Kolchak was one of the last to leave on 14 November, just hours ahead of the enemy. Seven trains accompanied him, carrying the imperial gold and his special convoy of Supreme Ruler bodyguards.

All Siberia seemed to be moving with him. Over 300 trains crowded with soldiers, families, Allied officials and military personnel, White sympathizers, businessmen, and members of the administration headed east, ostensibly for Irkutsk and safety. Thousands, unable to find a place, rode sledges along the ancient highway known as the Sibirsky Trakt. Though exact numbers will never be known, over 150,000 refugees, civilian and military, moved east into the endless forest *taiga* on a nightmare odyssey that would span four months. Only 70 of the trains would reach Irkutsk.

Immediately behind marched the armed forces: the 1st Army under General Anatoly Pepelyaev in the vanguard, the 2nd and 3rd Armies under Kappel and Voitsekhovsky acting as rearguard on each side of the Trans-Siberian. The Red 5th Army maintained steady pressure on the rear and occasionally company or battalion-sized actions broke out. More dangerous, however, were the 80,000–100,000 partisans that had become increasingly active since the late summer of 1919.

Conditions worsened in December as temperatures plunged deep below zero. Typhus struck and infected thousands. Trains lurched forward, stopped for hours or days, lurched again, then stopped again. Only trains designated 'first priority' by the Czech Legion could continue down the line immediately, 'second priority' having to await unfolding events. Trains needing fuel or repairs were shunted to a sideline, indefinitely.

Finally, an immense bottleneck of trains stacked up at Krasnoyarsk. Only a few would ever transit beyond this city, which had become a virtual graveyard of rolling stock. So too had it become a cemetery for the refugees. Forty thousand victims of typhus lay stranded in the rail yards of the ice-bound city. Entire trains rested immobile with their

Retreat in winter. (Czech Legion painting, 1926.)

frozen dead. For those yet to die, supplies dwindled until a loaf of bread became priceless – or the supreme gift of love.

By January the situation had become desperate. On the 8th, advance parties of the 5th Army overran the Allied Polish and Romanian garrison troops at Krasnoyarsk who had not been able to escape. Emboldened by the plight of the retreating columns, partisan chieftains closed like hungry wolves upon a wounded quarry. Trains and sledges were attacked as the 'Forest Brethren' rode in among the flanks.

White units, if poorly led, disintegrated. Other units, in platoons or companies, fought heroically to the last man. Kappel remained, holding the rearguard with the best of the troops, but by mid-January his legs were so frostbitten that he could no longer ride his horse. Refusing a place in the trains in order to command the troops by sledge, he died of exposure and pneumonia on the 26th. Voitsekhovsky assumed command.

Meanwhile, on 23 December, a revolt of Socialist Revolutionaries formed the 'Political Centre' in Irkutsk and brought Kolchak's administration to an end. No longer possessing a base, the Supreme Ruler abdicated on 4 January 1920, appointing Ataman Semenov commander-in-chief of White forces in Siberia and the Far East. Understanding the dangers ahead, he discharged his bodyguards and those closest to him. His long-time love, Madame Temireva, however, refused to leave his side. New guards from the Legion's 6th Regiment came on board and Allied flags were hoisted as symbols of protection.

Finally, on 7 January, his train reached the suburbs of Irkutsk. Under orders from the Legion commander, General Syrovy, his escort handed him over to agents of the Political Centre. General Janin, commander-in-chief of the Legion and the officer directed by the Allies to protect Kolchak, already had moved east towards Vladivostok, making himself unavailable for comment. The deal had been simple and pragmatic: Kolchak and the imperial gold in exchange for the free transit of the Legion and peace. Kolchak and

Temireva assumed their places in separate cells in the local prison.

Then, bowing to the inevitable, the Political Centre surrendered its authority to a Bolshevik Revolutionary Committee (REVKOM) on 20 January. Kolchak's trial began the next day and lasted until 6 February. According to the testimony of one of his interrogators and the transcripts of the proceedings, he behaved with 'dignity'.

Voitsekhovsky, meanwhile, had brought the main army through, overpowering Bolshevik-controlled towns, rail stations and nests of partisans where possible, or bypassing them when not. Arriving at Irkutsk on 3 February, he demanded Kolchak's release. Preliminary skirmishing began in the suburbs two days later.

Lenin had desired a spectacular show trial of the Supreme Ruler in Moscow, complete with select members of the press. The Whites' arrival at Irkutsk, however, upped the stakes. Facing the imminence of Kolchak's rescue, the Bolsheviks determined on a more expedient action. In the early hours before dawn on 7 February, special agents of REVKOM removed Kolchak to the banks of the Angara River where a hole had been prepared in the ice. Refusing their blindfold, Kolchak died as he had lived, bravely and without compromise.

Sensibly refusing to sack Irkutsk in revenge as some of the Whites counselled, Voitsekhovsky instead marched the army into Manchuria. In April 1920 he reorganized those units that had survived into three parts: the 1st Corps, 2nd Corps and 3rd Corps, consisting of, respectively, 11,000, 5,000 and 6,500 men. A further 10,000 non-combatants were in tow. These survivors would become known as the *Kappelevtsi* in honour of their fallen hero. Many of these troops continued resistance in the Maritime province surrounding Vladivostok until autumn 1922 when the Red Army took possession of the Far Eastern seaboard.

Some went on to serve in the armies of the Chinese warlords, one unit commanding an armoured train group in action during

A case in Soviet propaganda
This photo supposedly portrays atrocities committed by the Asiatic Cavalry
Division, commanded by Russia's 'Bloody Baron', General Baron Roman Fedorovich
Ungern-Sternberg in 1920. Three versions of this photo exist, the correct, original
one and two edited versions with clipped and worn edges and 'period' handwriting
superimposed to create a certain 'authenticity'. One of the doctored versions places the
alleged event in Manchuria-Mongolia, while a second captions the Urals. One photo,
compliments of the Soviet Novosti Press, found its way into Chamberlain's highly
acclaimed history of the Russian Revolution and both false variants are now widely
available from European photo archives.

The original and true photo, however, dates to 1912, eight years before the alleged
'atrocity'. Two American travellers, Richardson L. Wright and Bassett Digby, collected the
photo while reporting on 'Execution Day', an annual event held in the city of Tsitsitcar in
Central Manchuria. During this period, the Russians and Chinese jointly administered the
railways in Manchuria. The photo in question actually depicts Hung-Huse bandits caught
and beheaded by the Chinese for raiding the rails.

Chinese officials traditionally delivered the severed heads of criminals to the Russian
consulate as proof that justice had been done, after which the heads were returned. These
Russian consulate officers have posed for the photo: five appear stern, two are laughing
and one pretends deep, pensive thought – humorous, or tasteless – depending on one's
own predilections – but not a White Army atrocity. (*Through Siberia: an Empire in the
Making*, New York: McBride, Nast & Company, 1913)

the 1920s. Many eventually settled into the
Russian communities at Harbin or Shanghai.

Even then, their displacement saw no
end. At the conclusion of World War Two,
the Red Army advanced into Manchuria,
causing the Whites to evacuate Harbin.
The same fate awaited the community at
Shanghai during the Chinese communist
takeover in 1948. The author's father, serving
in the US Navy during the Chinese Civil
War, befriended one White gentleman
reduced to playing the piano in a hotel bar.

White resistance continued sporadically
in other corners of the Far East from 1920
to 1922. Sickened by his brutality, the
Ussuri Cossacks revolted against Ataman I.
M. Kalmykov in 1920. Eventually
apprehended crossing the border into
China, he was shot by Chinese guards
while 'trying to escape'. His mentor,
Ataman G. M. Semenov of the Trans-Baikal
Cossacks, who by all accounts ran an
almost equally barbarous regime, went into
exile when his supporters, the Japanese,

Red partisan leader N. A. Kalandarishvili, nicknamed 'Dedushka' or 'Grandad'. This Georgian Anarchist led partisan bands in the Baikal region against the Czechs and Kolchak's Whites in 1918–19. In 1920 he transferred his depredations to the Japanese, finally being killed in action against the remnants of the Whites in Yakutsk in 1922. (Sovietsky Kudoshnik art card, 1966)

evacuated the Russian Far East on 25 October 1922.

Another protégé of Semenov, General Baron Roman von Ungern-Sternberg, attempted to resurrect the empire of Genghis Khan in Mongolia in 1920–21. A former cavalry officer turned Buddhist mystic and sadist, the 'Bloody Baron' or 'Mad Baron', as his admirers and critics knew him, formed the Asiatic Cavalry Division, a collection of several thousand irregulars with whom he intended to purge Russia of Bolshevism. After several

Vasily Konstantinovich Blyukher. In the opening months of 1918, he commanded the South Urals Partisan Army, a force of 10,000 that carried a red banner with white skull and crossbones. In these days, Blyukher fought against Ataman Dutov's Cossacks and according to Soviet hagiography, wore a 'black mask'. He became the first recipient of the Order of the Red Banner after his forces broke through enemy lines near Samara in September 1918. He went on to play an instrumental part in the defeat of Kolchak's Siberians in 1919–20 and a critical role in breaching the White Army's defences at Perekop, Crimea in 1920. (Photo card, Planeta, 1972)

battles and an abortive invasion of Manchuria, he was betrayed by one of his Mongol 'princes' into the hands of the Reds on 22 August 1921. After a brief if politically calculated show trial in which he casually pleaded 'guilty' to all crimes, he was executed by firing squad in Novonikolaevsk, Siberia, on 15 September.

The last of the White crusaders, General Anatoly Pepelyaev, undertook an amazingly quixotic gamble from January to June 1923, landing by sea in distant Yakutsk with the 'Siberian Volunteer Corps' which he had created from the more adventurous elements in Vladivostok and Harbin. Pepelyaev was an experienced soldier, having commanded armies under the Provisional Siberian Government in 1918, then Kolchak in 1919. Setting out in the dense, snowy *taiga*, his forlorn hope of 5,000 former regulars fought several sharp engagements with the Red Army before being broken and finally captured on 17 June.

The Ukraine

The UHA had ceased to exist by April 1920. In order to continue the struggle against the Bolsheviks and establish the UNR on Ukrainian soil, Petlyura concluded an alliance with Poland in April. In exchange for military assistance, the UNR accepted the loss of Galicia. Directory troops numbering 23,000 advanced with the Poles in the offensive that took Kiev on 5 July 1920 during the Russo-Polish War. However, the ensuing Red counter-attack eliminated all gains, and the armistice in October between Poland and the Bolsheviks required the internment of the UNR army.

In March 1921 the Treaty of Riga divided the Ukraine between the Russian Soviet Federated Socialist Republic, the Ukrainian Soviet Socialist Republic and Poland. The last of the Directory's troops conducted partisan raids into the Ukraine in November, but these bands were surrounded and destroyed by Red cavalry.

Red dawn

The Red Army pursued Denikin nearly 800 kilometres, arriving, exhausted, at Rostov in January. There, in early February, the Caucasus Army Group was established, consisting of the 8th, 9th, 10th and 11th Armies and the 1st Horse Army under the overall command of Tukachevsky. Only a third of the combined ration strength of 215,000 were combatants, including 23,000 cavalry. The 1st Horse Army, having completed formation in mid-November 1919, had led the way. With 15,000 cavalry, 19 pieces of artillery and eight armoured trains, it was now a formidable tool of war.

These forces completed the defeat of the southern Whites in April and extended their operations into the Caucasus. The civil war seemed over.

Suddenly, however, Poland began advancing into the Ukraine on 25 April. Understanding that Denikin, if victorious, had intended to reincorporate their country into a new (White) Russian Empire, the Poles had waited until his destruction before beginning their own offensive. Polish troops entered Kiev on 6 May. Not intending to occupy the Ukraine indefinitely, but merely to round out their borders, the Poles were counting on the Directory forces of Petlyura, with whom they were in alliance, to raise a large Ukrainian army in support against the Reds. In the end, they were disappointed.

The Bolsheviks, on the other hand, had long-term plans for the Ukraine. Believing themselves attacked by the Allies through their surrogates, the Poles, they determined to reconquer the Ukraine and then advance into Poland. In the Bolshevik worldview, the conquest of Poland might conceivably lead to a general revolution throughout Europe. As for the Allies, they had indeed been supplying Poland, but were taken completely by surprise by the invasion themselves.

Two Red Army groups formed in response. Pushing Petlyura and the Poles out of Kiev on 12 June, they prepared for the invasion of Poland itself. Egorov, commanding the Southwest Army Group, consisting of (from north to south) the 14th, 1st Horse and 12th Armies, moved south of the Pripet Marshes on Lvov. The Western Army Group, under Tukachevsky, contained (from north to south) the 4th, 15th, 3rd and 16th Armies. Tukachevsky advanced north of the Pripet Marshes on Warsaw. Owing to the immense barrier posed by the marshes, the groups acted independently. After major successes, both groups were repulsed, failing to take their end objectives.

In a major patriotic outpouring against the Red invasion, the Poles had assembled an army of 740,000, counting militia, reserves and non-combatants. The head of the Polish Army, General Joseph Pilsudsky,

counter-attacked Tukachevsky from the Vistula River line near Warsaw in August. Both sides opened diplomatic talks that led to an armistice on 12 October.

Meanwhile, a weakened 13th Army had stood against a White resurgence in the south, in the Crimea. In September, Mikhail Frunze began preparing the assault on the Whites' positions on the Dnieper River line in the Northern Tauride. Under his command was the newly established Southern Army Group. By the end of October, five armies were concentrated against Wrangel in a 400-kilometre arc: (from west to east) the 6th Army, the 1st and 2nd Horse Armies, then the 4th and 13th Armies. These armies contained the highest number of Bolshevik Party members yet seen in a Red campaign, approximately one in eight, a proportion high enough to be classed, by their own accounting, as 'elite'.

Frunze's main strategy involved pinning the Whites along the eastern Tauride long enough for the 1st Horse Army to cut a swathe across their rear and sever their retreat into the Crimea. The majority of White forces would be caught in the open and annihilated. Failing to block the Whites from retreating into the Crimea, Frunze had no choice but a battle of attrition.

For the main attack on the Turkish Wall at Perekop, Frunze chose Vasily Blyukher's elite 51st Division, a division that had well proven itself against Kolchak. To achieve extra firepower, Blyukher fielded one machine gun for every 17 men. Just before this attack, the cavalry component of the 51st crossed the Sivash Marshes on the night of 7/8 November along with the 15th and 52nd Rifle Divisions. According to Anarchist literature, Makhno's elite *tachanka* machine-gun regiment also crossed, an event that later Soviet history chose to ignore. Success in both sectors, at Perekop and the Sivash, resulted in the enemy's evacuation of the Crimea and the end of the major campaigns between Red and White.

The growth of the Red Army had been phenomenal in 1920. By October, the ration strength stood at 5,498,000. Only 1,780,000,

however, were at the front and of these only half a million were combat effectives. Approximately 159,000 were in the Labour Army, 391,000 in the Reserve Army, while half a million served in transportation, railway and administrative departments. A further 2,600,000 were stationed in the rear in military districts. These could be called upon for a host of duties pursuant to achieving a new 'socialist' future.

Reds at Kakhovka stand triumphantly beside a captured Mark V tank, autumn 1920. Painting by F. G. Krichevsky. (Soviet art card, c. 1934)

Consolidation and the Second Civil War, 1921–22

The end of the Whites meant the Reds were able to round out their borders at the expense of their neighbours. In the west, they accepted the loss of Finland, Poland and the Baltic states. In 1920, they signed treaties with Estonia in February, with Lithuania in July, Latvia in August and Finland in October. A treaty with Poland followed in March 1921. These losses were temporary, however. From 1939 to 1945, Poland and the Baltic states were 'returned to the fold'. After the conclusion of World War Two in 1945, Red hegemony extended into

Czechoslovakia, Hungary, Romania and Bulgaria, regions about which not even the tsars had dreamed.

Bolshevik power gradually extended eastward to the Pacific Ocean. The Red Army invaded Manchuria and Mongolia in 1920–21. The month after the Japanese evacuation of Vladivostok in October 1922, the Bolsheviks annexed the Far Eastern Republic, thereby removing the last of their political obstacles in the east.

In the south, the Red Army took possession of the Caucasus region between the Black and Caspian Seas. The Reds entered Azerbaijan in April 1920 and Armenia that December. Georgia fell in February 1921.

Advances in the southeast, in Central Asia, were more problematical. A 'Basmachi Revolt' had begun in 1918 to counter Bolshevik food requisitions. Further, traditional Islam had little in common with the political and cultural aspects of Bolshevism. The revolt spread to include those interested in a 'pan-Turkish' union, hearkening to the days

Red troops crossing the treacherous Sivash salt marshes in the Crimea under fire, November 1920. (Painting by N. S. Samokish, art card c. 1920s)

when the Turkish tribes maintained affiliations, and even to those espousing the formation of a single pan-Islamic state. Former 'Young Turk' head of state Enver Pasha, in exile after World War One, joined the Basmachis in 1921 and died in August of the following year while leading a cavalry charge against the Reds. The Red Army broke the back of the rebels in 1922, although resistance continued until 1934 when the last of the Basmachis were captured.

More dangerous in the eyes of Lenin, however, were the internal rebellions that questioned the foundation of Bolshevism itself – insurrections that the Red leadership privately referred to as the 'Second Civil War'. Fortunately for the Bolsheviks, these revolts occurred after the main battle fronts of the civil war had been silenced. The Red Army had more than enough men to extend the borders of the Russian Soviet Federated Socialist Republic while simultaneously crushing internal opponents.

Politically, the Bolsheviks could not consolidate power until they had fully suppressed internal dissidents. Elements considered 'bourgeois' or remnants of the

White Armies were identified, rounded up, then shot or sent to labour camps such as the notorious Cheka establishment at the Solovetsky Monastery complex at Archangel. Socialist Revolutionaries, Anarchists and Mensheviks who had failed to see a deep enough red in the light of revolution were identified and 'processed' in the same way by the end of 1922. So too were the various groups of partisans who were unable to adapt to the new political way of life or accept the loss of the freedoms they had known during the civil war. Battles with outlying partisans groups, labelled according to formula as 'bandits', lasted through the 1920s in Siberia.

The rebellion at the naval base of Kronstadt from 28 February to 18 March 1921 was a particularly embarrassing matter because the sailors of the Baltic Fleet had been at the heart of the Revolution from the very beginning. Their demands, addressed to the Bolshevik Party, included new elections to the soviets, the rights of free assembly and free speech, the freedom to establish trade unions, the freeing of socialist political prisoners and the equalization of rations. In short, they asked for a limitation of state centrism and a return of the freedoms for which they had fought.

In response, the Bolsheviks decided to take Kronstadt by storm before the ice surrounding the island naval base could

Red commander Efim Ivanovich Kurashov, by L. F. Golovanov, wearing the new 1922 pattern uniform. (Soviet art card)

melt. On 7 March, Trotsky ordered Tukachevsky and 60,000 troops to begin operations. Over the next 11 days the sailors fought fiercely, inflicting 10,000 casualties on the Red Army before being defeated. Of the approximately

14,000 sailors at Kronstadt, about half managed to escape to Finland. The other half died in battle, were executed after the fact or served out their days in labour camps.

Equally disturbing were the peasant rebellions on the Volga, in Siberia and in the province of Tambov. These revolts were the inexorable consequence of the Bolsheviks' need to requisition food for their cities and the natural desire of the peasantry to retain as much food as possible on home ground. Many rebels also asked for freedoms similar to those the Kronstadt sailors had demanded.

The most virulent rebellion broke out on 19 August 1920 at Tambov, 500 kilometres southeast of Moscow. By October, 50,000 rebels were in the field under the command of Alexander Antonov. Organized into regiments, the rebels created their own uniforms and insignia and thrashed every Red expedition sent out to obtain food.

Freed from operations at Kronstadt, the Reds were able to transfer 32,500 infantry, 8,000 cavalry and special-purpose Cheka detachments, all under the command of Tukachevsky, to Tambov in March 1921. Every available technological arm was employed, from machine guns and artillery to armoured trains, armoured cars and aircraft, to poison gas. Aircraft rained gas on rebel forest strongholds during the summer and autumn of 1921. Families and whole villages associated with the rebellion were displaced into specially constructed concentration camps. Nearly a quarter of a million died in the conflagration. Antonov and the last of his commanders were executed in June 1922.

Meanwhile, the Red Army crushed Makhno's popular insurgent army in the Ukraine in August 1921. In Bolshevik terms, these Anarchists had been no more than 'debauched bandits'.

Forced and uncompensated food requisitions and the general economic dislocations caused by the civil war contributed to the famines of 1920–23 that occurred on the Volga, in Armenia, the Crimea and the Ukraine. These events further exacerbated peasant unrest and

Sailors of the Baltic Sea Fleet based at Kronstadt. True to their revolutionary ideals, they demanded greater freedoms and equality and were ruthlessly crushed by the Bolsheviks in 1921. (Museum of the Revolution art card, 1933)

undermined general faith in the economic system known as 'war communism'. Always pragmatic, Lenin promulgated a different economic strategy known as the New Economic Policy (NEP) on 21 March 1921. NEP temporarily relaxed collectivization policies and allowed small private farms and business to operate, even while the apparatus of state centrism continued otherwise unchecked. NEP incentives ended drastically when Stalin announced the advent of the Five Year Plans in 1928.

The Russian Soviet Federated Socialist Republic lasted until 30 December 1921, thereafter becoming known as the Union of Soviet Socialist Republics. The new name reflected the increasing consolidation and control that became a hallmark of Soviet society.

A Century Redrawn

No one has been able to calculate accurately the cost in human life attributable to the civil war. Reasoned estimates have placed the number of dead from battle and disease in the Red Army as low as 425,000 and as high as 1,213,000. Numbers for their opponents range from 325,000 to 1,287,000. Another 200,000–400,000 died in prison or were executed as a result of the 'Red Terror' against 'enemies of the people'. A further 50,000 may have been victims of the corresponding 'White Terror'. Another 5 million are believed to have died in the ensuing famines of 1921–22, directly caused by the economic disruption of revolution and civil war. The number of civilians succumbing to the epidemics of typhus, typhoid and cholera in 1918–21 and to the Spanish influenza pandemic of 1918–19 can only be imagined. The final butcher's bill totalled 7–14 million.

This death list doubles if one considers the forces unleashed by the Red victory at the end of the civil war: the forcible collectivization of agriculture, the travails of the Five Year Plans with their attendant labour camps, and the political and military purges under Stalin in the 1930s. Moreover, much of the former empire's human talent – intellectuals, doctors, actors, artists, musicians, administrators and scientists – emigrated to join the Russian diaspora during and after the civil war period. This number alone has been estimated from 2–3.5 million.

The prospects for a Bolshevik victory in the civil war hung in the balance in 1918–19, but were much more certain in 1920–21. Above all, the Reds held the centre ground, central Russia, the heartland, with all the advantages that that position conferred. Here lay the old tsarist stocks of war, the primary arms factories, the thickest net of railways and the largest population. The Bolsheviks could readily reinforce their fronts from a central manpower base, or shift forces from one front to another according to need.

This population base became increasingly important as the civil war dragged on. From May 1918 to December 1920, the Red Army grew from an approximate fighting strength of 300,000 to 800,000. A further 900,000 formed the second line of reserves. During these two-and-a-half years, nearly 5.5 million personnel had been registered for mobilization. These either passed through the ranks of the Red Army, worked in labour armies, maintained internal security or deserted. According to some assessments,

Russian girl, victim of the devastating famine that resulted from civil war. (Belgian Red Cross photocard, c. 1921, Bullock collection)

The Whites continued to dream about returning to a Russia free of Bolshevism. In this illustration, soldiers of the Armed Forces of South Russia, including members of the Markov, Kornilov and Drozdovsky Divisions, finally reach the Kremlin in Moscow. (Chasevoi, 1932)

approximately half of the Red forces deserted during these years.

Nevertheless, larger reserves meant that the Reds could establish training centres in the rear and keep their students under technical instruction and political indoctrination longer than could the Whites. Second- or third-rate troops might be a

liability on the main battle front, but they could still guard bridges and railways against partisans or rebellious peasants, organize chairs for military classrooms or requisition food from the local populace.

Nevertheless, the Whites were never able to conscript and field comparable numbers. Denikin's AFSR reached its peak on the Southern Front in autumn 1919 with 98,000 combatants, including the Cossacks, and 46,000 in reserve (the British Military Mission calculated this latter number at 136,000). Opposed to the AFSR were a total of 677,000 Reds in the Southern and

Southeastern Army Groups, of which 148,000 were front-line fighters.

This numerical inequality occurred on other fronts as well. Yudenich's Northwestern Army reached its peak in autumn 1919 with 20,000 combatants. Against this threat, the Reds were able to poise 73,000 soldiers. Kolchak fielded perhaps 137,000 front-line troops in March 1919. Overall, White forces in the east, at least on paper and including a high proportion of non-combatants, rose from 160,000 in November 1918 to 450,000 in June 1919. A large number of these Volga and Siberian conscripts never received arms or saw military service. Many of those that did deserted in the summer and autumn of 1919. Opposed to Kolchak, the Red Eastern Army Group had 361,000 combatant and support troops, with 195,000 in the Volga region in reserve.

An exhaustive, statistical study about what these numbers actually meant and how they translated onto the battlefield has yet to be written. However, it is clear enough that the Bolsheviks had a significantly larger pool from which to draw. Barring an internal revolt or collapse, time was on the side of the Reds.

These human resources varied greatly in value. Russia remained overwhelmingly agrarian in 1918, and conscription, to which all sides resorted, meant drafting peasants. No political faction found the peasantry enthusiastic about military service. Few peasants had the literacy or political prescience to care about which side won, merely that they retained the land already gained in the revolutionary seizures of 1917–18. Forced to choose, most considered the Whites, with their complicated land reform policies, the greater threat. Red promises were 'now'. Few could foresee the loss of their land to the new landlord, the Soviet state itself.

On the other side were those who understood the stakes, and were willing to make sacrifices for them. These were the minority, the elite, those who were willing to kill and be killed. While numbers could and did make the difference, as in the campaign

for the Crimea in 1920, all too often it was the élan of the shock troops of a particular faction, reinforced with automatic rifles and machine guns and led by charismatic commanders, that dominated the Field of Mars. The Whites arguably attracted the best of the old army and created additional elite units over time. Except for the Latvians, who had entered the conflict with discipline and experience, other Red formations, such as Chapaev's 25th Regiment, Blyukher's 51st and several units of the *Konarmiya*, had to earn 'elite' status under fire. The civil war was won on the battlefield by the side that could recruit, logistically sustain, and replace a larger number of *committed* forces.

Unlike the disparate White armies, the Reds had a central command, and if there were discordant voices, these were brought under control and a common strategy prevailed, even if this strategy later proved in error. The Bolshevik Party, headed by a leader generally accepted by all, Lenin, provided steady if imperfect direction. Trotsky, architect of the Red Army, embraced Lenin's leadership. Propaganda departments maintained consistent and easy-to-understand themes. The internal security services, the Cheka, led by Dzerzhinsky, remained loyal and were utterly ruthless in suppressing dissidents, whether real or imagined.

Perhaps studied least by historians were the tens of thousands of lower- and middle-grade officers, officials, party members and agitators who risked or sacrificed their lives for the hope of a new tomorrow. Legends, heroes and heroines aside, these were the more mundane yet critical cadres who fought and fell without an Order of the Red Banner fixed to their chests, who took a final breath on some forgotten corner of a battlefield, or carried out conscientious work behind a neglected desk in a scarcely remembered sector, but who nevertheless *believed*. This was the cement that built the Revolution.

The Whites had certain advantages of their own. In a conflict where mobility could be a critical factor, they had superior cavalry, both in quality and quantity, on their Southern and even Eastern Fronts. This condition lasted through autumn 1919 until both White fronts were forced into their arduous and ultimately disastrous retreats. This tide had turned by the New Year, 1920. In the 1980s, Guards Cavalry veteran Nicholas Volkov-Mouromtsoff held extensive interviews with the author during which he described the massed cavalry battle of Egorlykskaia against Budenny's *Konarmiya* in February 1920. In his own words, 'These Red cavalry had been completely equal to us in quality.'

Blessed with an abundance of officers who were technically competent, the Whites could usually outmanoeuvre their opponents, face down superior numbers, exact greater discipline and steadiness from their units and manage their artillery, aircraft, armoured trains, tanks and armoured cars to better effect. These tactical advantages remained throughout 1919 in the case of the Northwestern Army and throughout 1920 on the Southern Front.

Overall, however, the Whites failed to establish a comprehensive social and political programme that could be understood by the masses. Themes of personal sacrifice, exhortations to sign up for military service for Mother Russia and fight for the geographical unity of their country only inspired a few – too few. Many of those who might have been expected to respond to these pleas and support the Whites had been killed in World War One, the last of them in the shock units that led the offensives of 1917. Thus they entered the civil war with a depleted force.

Further, each of the White fronts had the misfortune of being based on the peripheries of the Russian heartland. For Denikin's Volunteer Army this meant that cooperation with and concessions to his Cossack hosts was vital. For most of its existence, Yudenich's Northwestern Army had to be based on the foreign soil of Estonia. Miller's Northern Army and Kolchak's Siberian Army were located in areas where the people looked at the civil war with an almost completely indifferent eye. They had not yet tasted the full impact of Bolshevism. Moreover, the northern region had few inhabitants. Kolchak had the additional disadvantage of having his

entire rear area in the hands of the Allies and the Czechs whom he could not command, and the Cossack warlords whom he could not control. These facts placed limitations on the courses of action available to the White leadership.

These fronts were separated by hundreds of miles and lacked any means of direct communication. Consequently, the fronts never joined and one White offensive was unable to act synchronously with another. Thus, when Denikin advanced in 1919, Kolchak's forces already were in retreat. Yudenich did manage to time his move against Petrograd at the height of Denikin's advance on Moscow, but his knowledge of conditions and positions on the Southern Front were vague and his own forces were too few. Moreover, the Whites, unlike the Reds, could not transition their best or elite troops from front to front where they were needed most.

On a more subtle, psychological level, the Whites also were at a disadvantage. Although the majority of the younger White commanders easily adapted to the new methods of war, as did the best of their Red counterparts, the Whites were more bound to tradition and accepted standards of war. Prisoners could be whipped or brought in roped to a Cossack horse or summarily executed, villages could be pillaged, and women occasionally raped. Yet, with the exceptions of the brutal White warlords in the Far East, at no time did the 'White Terror' equal the sheer volume or pervasiveness of the 'Red Terror' or their methods approach the barbarous nature exacted by some units of the Red Army and the Cheka.

All too often, constitutional niceties, and traditional standards of behaviour prevailed. In his memoirs, Wrangel lamented that he had not been able to find enough labour to strengthen his critical Crimean defenses in 1920. Conscripting the population into labour armies, as the Reds did, habitually, seems never to have occurred to him. In early 1920, Wrangel rhetorically asked General Mai-Maevsky about the difference between White and Red and received a telling reply:

'Is not the whole difference simply that the Bolshevists have not scrupled about their means, and therefore have gained the upper hand?'

Allied intervention turned out to be a mixed blessing. Intervention did bolster the morale of White units and administrations, and did convey a sense of legitimacy. Britain, France and the United States sent large shipments of supplies to the Whites; however, substantial munitions and equipment did not begin arriving until spring 1919, and the majority did not reach the White fronts until summer. The Whites, therefore, accomplished much in the early period on their own. Military aid, of course, was beneficial, and quite necessary, given the much larger Red industrial capacity. At the same time, the Allies used their superior naval forces to impose an economic blockade on the Red centre.

Allied action against the anti-White forces was always peripheral – in the Far East, in the Caspian, in the far north and against the Red Navy and shore forts along the Baltic. American and Japanese units cooperated against large formations of Red partisans in the Far East, but only in the north, on the Murmansk and Archangel Fronts, did Allied military units openly engage regular units of the Red Army on a sustained basis. However, for political as well as geographical reasons, these northern fronts either failed to capture Petrograd or link with the forces of Admiral Kolchak. Instructors attached to the Allied Military Missions, of course, did provide training on various hardware, including tanks, aircraft, machine guns and artillery. Not a few became ardent supporters of the White cause, engaging the enemy, if against official orders, when the opportunity arose.

One perennial question is whether direct and forceful Allied intervention could have overturned Bolshevism. The obvious answer is of course *yes*, at least militarily and immediately. If the British had landed 50,000 men in the Baltic in autumn 1919, coordinated with Yudenich, encouraged the Estonians to expand their contribution, and/or influenced Finland to attack Petrograd

from the north, the Bolshevik seat of revolution would have fallen. Miller could have pushed his reliable troops south from Lake Onega, Kolchak could have regained the Urals or Volga and Denikin and the Cossacks could have delivered the crushing blow to the Bolshevik administrative capital, Moscow.

But this historical 'what if' was not to be. Worn out in World War One, eager to demobilize and return to a peacetime footing, confused by the plethora of international challenges wanting solutions in the post-war environment, the Allies talked, prevaricated, then sent supplies and munitions, and finally condolences. Few, the gallant Winston Churchill and the ardent US Ambassador Francis aside, yet understood the full ramifications of Bolshevism.

On the other hand, Allied intervention allowed Bolshevik agitators to hammer home the message that Russia had been invaded and to adopt the position that they were the true defenders of the homeland. Posters depicted the Whites as puppets of the Allies, vicious hirelings of international capital. Intervention allowed the Bolsheviks to dodge the very important and embarrassing fact that there had been considerable internal opposition to their policies. The impact of this propaganda increased from the 1920s and continued at least into the early 1980s, bolstering the Soviet position during the Cold War that the West had invaded Russia, not the other way around. In its crudest form, resistance to Soviet authority had been nothing more than actions paid for by the imperialists.

The Russian Civil War profoundly affected the remainder of the 20th century. Red victory unleashed a doctrine that was international in intent and bent on directly challenging the methods of capitalism, democracy and the general world order. By the end of World War Two, the Soviets were in a sufficiently strong military, economic and geographical position to promote communist revolutions worldwide, from Eastern Europe to China and Southeast Asia to Africa and the Caribbean. These revolutions led them directly into

ПСЫ АНТАНТЫ.

ДЕНИКИН   КОЛЧАК   ЮДЕНИЧ

ABOVE The civil war set the stage for the future Cold War. Here the Americans, French and British are portrayed as hound-masters with the dogs Denikin, Kolchak and Yudenich on leash. Soviet leaders could always assert, truthfully, that the Western powers had occupied their soil. (Soviet art card, c. 1919)

BELOW A less-than-flattering Soviet depiction of Allied Intervention in North Russia. The Americans herd Bolshevik sympathizers toward a staff car. Inside sits an aged White general and a stern British officer. Surrounding the car are White officers, the one just to the left wearing the Russian national colours of red, blue and white on a strip of cloth affixed diagonally on his hat. (Painting by P. P. Sokolov-Skalia, Soviet art card, c. 1920s)

confrontation with the West in a nearly half-century period known as the Cold War.

The civil war exacted a deadly toll on its participants. Casualties among the White leadership were severe. Among the field officers, it was not uncommon for the proportion of wounded and killed in action to exceed 50–90 per cent, depending on the particular unit, front and year. Deaths among the senior commanders that can be attributed to battle action, illness contracted while on campaign, or execution by the Bolsheviks included Kornilov, Markov and Alexiev in 1918, Drozdovsky in 1919, Mai-Maevsky, Kolchak, Kalmykov, Romanovsky and Kappel in 1920, and von Ungern-Sternberg in 1921.

In exile, the Whites continued to dream of returning to Russia with an army to overthrow communism. They kept contacts and maintained paramilitary formations under arms until the late 1920s and in cadet training schools throughout the 1930s. Meanwhile, the Soviets relentlessly pursued their enemies throughout the world, conducting a brutal war in the shadows from the 1920s until the end of the 1940s.

Bolshevik agents shot Dutov and Pokrovsky in the 1920s. Wrangel, according to his son Alexis, was slowly poisoned, and died in 1928. Kutepov and Miller were abducted and executed in the 1930s, while Pepelyaev, already in captivity, was shot.

P. Kotov's rendering of Semyon Konstantinovich Timoshenko during the civil war when he commanded a brigade in the 1st Horse Army. He became a Marshal of the Soviet Union in 1940 and fought in World War Two.

Many Soviet generals and political leaders into the 1960s, including Nikita Khrushchev and Alexei Kosygin, served in the civil war. (Central Museum of the Workers' and Peasants' Red Army art card, c. 1930)

Skoblin vanished in the tangled web of espionage that was Paris in those days. Evidence suggests he had been 'turned' then liquidated. Another source indicates he died a hero's death in the Spanish Civil War fighting the communists. The last of the diehards and their sons fought the Reds in World War Two. Semenov, Shkuro and Krasnov were captured and hanged by the Soviets in 1946–47.

A few survived these crucibles to live on relatively peacefully in exile. Bermondt-Avalov died in the United States, as did Denikin in 1947 and Kerensky in 1970. Dieterichs died in China in 1937, while Yudenich expired on the French Riviera that same year. Kolchak's love, Madame Temirova, reached France where she lived in obscurity and vanished from the historical record.

Similarly, the civil war thinned the ranks of the Red commanders. Two leaders killed in action, Nikolai Schors (Shchors in Ukrainian) and Vasily Chapaev, were immortalized in Soviet movies and therefore received international attention: *Schors* in 1939 and *Chapaev* in 1935. Chapaev died a hero under fire in 1919 before his rollicksome, independent ways could embarrass the future Soviet leadership. Other fallen commanders like Sivers or Markin generally would not be known outside the areas of the former Soviet Union.

Ironically, the greatest danger to former Bolshevik commanders lay not in the civil war but in its aftermath and from the very party and comrades they had served so loyally. Most died in the elaborately staged show trials of the 1930s, ordered by the Soviet Union's new dictator, Stalin, who intended to eliminate any conceivable competitors possessing ambition or talent. Frunze died first in 1925, mysteriously, during a stomach operation that had been recommended and arranged personally by Stalin. Vatsetis, whose Latvian Rifles arguably saved the Revolution, was accused of being a fascist and executed in 1938. Tukachevsky and Blyukher were brutally tortured prior to

their executions in 1937 and 1938. Egorov followed in 1939.

Many high-level Bolshevik political leaders also perished before, during and after the show trials. Lenin died in January 1924 due to medical complications resulting from the attempt on his life in July 1918. Before his death he warned colleagues against the growing power of Stalin, who had become Secretary of the Communist Party in April 1922. A political coup staged by Stalin forced Trotsky, whom many considered the natural successor to Lenin, into exile in 1928.

Thereafter, Trotsky's name became synonymous with 'fascist' and 'counter-revolutionary'. Stalin's judiciary accused victims of conspiring with Trotsky to commit crimes against the Soviet state in order to establish their 'guilt' during the kangaroo-court proceedings. Once the trials were over, Trotsky was no longer useful politically. A Soviet agent stabbed him to death with an ice pick at his house of exile in Mexico in 1940.

The political comradeship formed by Stalin, Voroshilov and Budenny during the sieges of Tsaritsyn in 1918–19 endured through World War Two to the end of their days. Stalin died in his bed in 1953, Voroshilov following in 1969 and Budenny in 1973. Several veterans of the civil war such as Zhukov, Timoshenko, Chuikov, Konev, and Rokossovksy, the first two having served in Budenny's 1st Horse Army, went on to receive important commands in World War Two. Two other veterans, Nikita Khrushchev and Alexei Kosygin, became key players on the world stage, Khrushchev as First Secretary of the Communist Party from 1953 to 1964, and Kosygin as Premier of the Soviet Union from 1964 to 1980.

Reconciliation between White and Red began in 1985 when Soviet President Mikhail Gorbachev promulgated the policies of *glasnost* (openness) and *perestroika* (reform). For the first time, Soviet scholars could begin coming to terms with the civil war and studying all sides without significant fear of political retaliation. They began reaching out to *émigré* communities and opening Western archives. This process accelerated throughout the 1990s after the fall of communism in Russia under the presidency of Boris Yeltsin. By the turn of the millennium, museums in Russia and the Ukraine had begun displays showcasing the former opponents of the Bolshevik regime: the Whites, the Ukrainian and other nationalist forces and even the Anarchists, including Nestor Makhno.

Interest in imperial Russia, after years of suppression, emerged and intensified. News that the remains of five members of the royal family had been discovered near Ekaterinburg (where they had been shot and butchered in July 1918) reached the Russian people in March 1991. On 17 July 1998, on the 80th anniversary of their deaths, the bodies of the tsar, tsarina and three of their daughters were buried in the St Peter and Paul Cathedral, St Petersburg. The remains of the last two members of the royal family would not be discovered until August 2007.

Finally, in the 21st century, the Whites started to come home. Russian citizens erected a statue to Admiral Kolchak in St Petersburg in 2002 and in Irkutsk in 2004. In 2005, the Irkutsk Brewery bottled and canned a spicy beer called 'Admiral Kolchak',

with the admiral's colour portrait on the label. A new movie, *Admiral Kolchak*, appeared in Russian theatres in 2008.

In October 2005, General Denikin's body was transferred from the St Vladimir Russian Cemetery in Jackson, New Jersey, USA, and interred in the Donskoi Monastery, Moscow. Shortly after, President Vladimir Putin approved the application of Marina Antonovna Denikina, the general's daughter, for citizenship in the new nationalist Russia. Then, in December 2006, forensic scientists discovered General Kappel's remarkably well-preserved remains in Harbin, China. These were transferred to the Donskoi Monastery in Moscow for reburial on 13 January 2007.

Today, Russia is a texture of symbols, memorials and statues that would have been recognizable to both Whites and Reds. Red flags have returned to the military, shorn of communist references, as have military patches and national flags with the former Russian tricolor. After briefly disappearing during the Yeltsin years, the old Soviet national anthem, one of the most inspiring in the world, is back, but with different words – words suggesting a new dawn, new unity and the healing of the old wounds of civil war.

Index

Visit the Osprey website

- Information about forthcoming books

- Author information

- Read extracts and see sample pages

- Sign up for our free newsletters

- Competitions and prizes